D0064707

Presented to:

_____

From:

_____

JESUS TODAY®

DEVOTIONS FOR KIDS

Sarah Young

Adapted by Tama Fortner

Edited by Kris Bearss

A Division of Thomas Nelson Publishers

Jesus Today®: Devotions for Kids

Published in Nashville, Tennessee, by Tommy Nelson. Tommy Nelson is an imprint of Thomas Nelson. Thomas Nelson is a registered trademark of HarperCollins Christian Publishing, Inc.

Tommy Nelson titles may be purchased in bulk for educational, business, fund-raising, or sales promotional use. For information, please e-mail SpecialMarkets@ThomasNelson.com.

Library of Congress Cataloging-in-Publication Data

Young, Sarah, 1946- author.
  Jesus today, devotions for kids : living every day with hope, living every day with Jesus / Sarah Young ; adapted by Tama Fortner ; edited by Kris Bearss.
    pages cm
  Audience: Ages 6-10.
  Summary: "With more than 800,000 units sold, Jesus Calling?: 365 Devotions for Kids shows that parents appreciate the opportunity to share the wisdom of Sarah Young's beloved writing with their children. Jesus TodayTM has sold more than 1 million copies since its release in 2012, making it the next huge success in the Jesus Calling? brand. Sarah Young has more than 14 million books in print. This kids' devotional follows in the footsteps of the massively successful Jesus Calling?: 365 Devotions for Kids and provides new content for children from Jesus Today, the 2013 ECPA Christian Book of the Year. This devotional will continue to expand Sarah Young's brand as it brings Scripture and encouragement to children. Jesus Today: Devotions for Kids is written as if Jesus Himself is assuring us that He is in control, that He is good, and that we can put our hope in Him."-- Provided by publisher.
  ISBN 978-0-7180-3805-2 (hardcover)
  1. Jesus Christ--Teachings--Juvenile literature. 2. Devotional exercises--Juvenile literature. 3. Devotional literature, American--Juvenile literature. 4. Christianity--21st century. I. Fortner, Tama, 1969- adapter. II. Bearss, Kris, editor. III. Title. IV. Title: Devotions for kids.
  BS2416.Y68 2016
  242.62--dc23
                                          2015024141

Printed in China

17 18 19 20 LEO 6 5 4 3

Mfr: LEO / Heshan, China / February 2017 / PO #9426516

Acknowledgments

I'd like to thank Tama Fortner for her excellent adaptation of *Jesus Today*—a very difficult assignment. I appreciate all the efforts of Jennifer Gott, my dedicated project manager, who skillfully guided this project in more ways than I can enumerate here. I'm very thankful for Kris Bearss, my longtime editor, who worked on this project with her usual expertise, diligence, and professionalism. Last, but definitely not least, I want to thank my creative publisher, Laura Minchew, for coming up with the idea for this book.

Introduction

Jesus Today: Devotions for Kids is about Jesus and His amazing Love for you. It's also a book about hope. Some kids may think that hoping is just wishful thinking. But the hope Jesus offers you is something you can hold on to—knowing it will never let you down. Because *Jesus* will never let you down! No matter what is happening—whether you are happy, scared, angry, or sad—God is always in control, and He is always good.

Like *Jesus Calling: 365 Devotions for Kids*, the devotions in this book are written as if Jesus is speaking right to you. I wrote the devotions this way to help you know that Jesus is with you all the time—the Friend who is always by your side. He knows everything about you, and He loves you more than you can imagine!

Jesus loves you *so much* that He died on the cross to take the punishment for your sins. If you have never asked Him to be your Savior—forgiving all your sins—I encourage you to do that very soon. It's the most important decision you will ever make! All the promises in the Bible are for *you* when Jesus is your Savior.

If you're a Christian, then your hope is strong and secure. Because Jesus has already paid for every one of your sins, you know you are completely forgiven. You also know that the story of your life in this world finishes wonderfully well—at the gates of heaven!

The Bible is the only perfect Word of God, and I've included Bible verses to go with each devotion. These verses from God's Word will help you learn how much Jesus loves you and why you can trust Him.

I hope you will find a quiet place to read these devotions slowly each day. Jesus loves spending time with you. And the better you get to know Him, the more you will love spending time with Him too. You can talk with Jesus about everything, wherever you are and whatever is happening. Remember: Jesus has *promised* to be with you always. And He hears every one of your prayers.

Sarah Young

What is hope?
Hope is expecting
God to keep His
promises . . .
and *knowing*
that He will.

God is not a man.
He will not lie.
God is not a human
being. He does not
change his mind.
What he says he
will do, he does.
What he promises,
he keeps.

—Numbers 23:19

My Kind of Hope

Put your hope in Me, because I love you . . . always.

Hope—*My* kind of hope—is very different from any other kind. It is more than a wish or a dream. It is *expecting* Me to keep My promises, because you *know* that I will. One of My greatest promises is to give you a happy ending to your story.

Yes, *your* story—because your life is a story. Put your hope in Me by trusting Me as your Savior and following Me. I promise that your adventure will end with a happily-ever-after in heaven with Me. I died on the cross so that you can have a forever like this!

No matter how tough this day may be, you can always have hope . . . because in *Me*, your story has an amazing ending. And knowing that will brighten even your darkest day.

So our hope is in the Lord. He is our help,
our shield to protect us. We rejoice in him.
We trust his holy name. Lord, show your
love to us as we put our hope in you.

—Psalm 33:20–22

That faith and that knowledge come from our
hope for life forever. God promised that life to
us before time began, and God does not lie.

—Titus 1:2

Not One Single Thing

Nothing can separate you from My Love.

Nothing you do or say or think will ever make Me stop loving you. It just isn't possible, because you're My precious one.

My Love is a gift. You don't have to earn it. You don't have to be perfect or even good enough. My Love is simply yours to keep. It secures your connection to Me—your Savior—forever.

So when everything is going well and you are happy, *enjoy it*. Don't worry about when the good might end or what troubles may come later. Just smile and thank Me! When things are tough, *be brave*! I will help you, I will never leave you, and I will love you no matter what.

This world will always have troubles. But there's one thing you never have to worry about, one thing you can always count on—My Love for you will never end!

Nothing above us, nothing below us, or
anything else in the whole world will ever
be able to separate us from the love of
God that is in Christ Jesus our Lord.

—Romans 8:39

"A thief comes to steal and kill and destroy. But
I came to give life—life in all its fullness."

—John 10:10

"I have told you these things so that you can have
peace in me. In this world you will have trouble.
But be brave! I have defeated the world!"

—John 16:33

My Plan

I have a perfect plan for your life.

But sometimes *My* plan might be different from yours. Sometimes it will involve doing something hard or uncomfortable, such as helping someone very different from you or being a friend to someone who is lonely. At other times My plan for you will include troubles and problems. That's not because I've stopped loving you. It's because I want you to learn to trust Me as we face those troubles together. When you're going through tough times, you need Me more than ever.

When My plan for you is different from what you expected, you can choose to be angry with Me. Or you can choose to trust that I want only what is best for you. Hard days won't last forever. Keep believing and hoping. Then, at just the right time, I will *lift you up*. Until then, *give Me all your worries*, and trust that My plan for you is *good*—because I love you.

"I know what I have planned for you," says the Lord. "I have good plans for you. I don't plan to hurt you. I plan to give you hope and a good future."

—Jeremiah 29:11

The Lord's love surrounds those who trust him.

—Psalm 32:10

Be joyful because you have hope. Be patient when trouble comes. Pray at all times.

—Romans 12:12

So be humble under God's powerful hand. Then he will lift you up when the right time comes. Give all your worries to him, because he cares for you.

—1 Peter 5:6–7

A Safe Place

A refuge is a safe place, a place to take shelter when storms come your way. I am your Refuge.

Storms aren't just rain, thunder, and lightning. They aren't just wind and hail or snow. They can also be worries and doubts, unkind words, problems at school, or troubles with parents or friends. No matter what storm you're facing, I will be your safe place, your Refuge.

When worries and fears creep into your thoughts, don't turn to the TV, the computer, the cell phone, or your favorite food. Turn to Me. Think about Me and My promises to always be with you and take care of you. When you choose to think about Me instead of your worries, you will find your shelter—in My Presence.

But it won't happen all by itself. You have to choose Me over your worries. When you do, your worries won't seem so worrisome anymore. There is Joy for *those who take refuge in Me*!

Control yourselves and be careful! The devil is your enemy. And he goes around like a roaring lion looking for someone to eat.

—1 PETER 5:8

Be merciful to me, God. Be merciful to me because I come to you for protection. I will come to you as a bird comes for protection under its mother's wings until the trouble has passed.

—PSALM 57:1

Taste and see that the LORD is good. Oh, the joys of those who take refuge in him!

—PSALM 34:8 NLT

Keep Asking

I am with you and within you, doing good things in your life. Even when you're not aware that I am with you, the Light of My Presence keeps shining brightly on you. And this Light has great Power! So dare to ask great things of Me. *I can do much, much more than anything you can ask or think of.* Nothing is impossible for Me.

Pray boldly, and keep praying in My name. Learn from the widow in the Bible who wouldn't give up. She went to the judge again and again, asking for what she needed. This judge *did not care about God* or *what people thought about him.* But because she kept asking, he finally gave her what she needed. If a selfish judge will do that, how much more will *I* give to My loved ones who *cry to Me night and day*!

You may have to wait for My answer—a little while or a long while. But don't quit praying! *Keep asking, and you will receive. Keep searching, and you will find.*

With God's power working in us, God can do much, much more than anything we can ask or think of.
—Ephesians 3:20

"Once there was a judge in a town. He did not care about God . . . [or] what people thought about him. In that same town there was a widow who kept coming to this judge. . . . But the judge did not want to help the widow. After a long time, he thought to himself. . . . 'This widow is bothering me. I will see that she gets her rights, or she will bother me until I am worn out!'" The Lord said, "Listen to what the bad judge said. God's people cry to him night and day. God will always give them what is right, and he will not be slow to answer them."
—Luke 18:2–8

"Yes, if a person continues asking, he will receive. If he continues searching, he will find. And if he continues knocking, the door will open for him."
—Luke 11:10

The Prince of Peace

I am the *Prince of Peace*. When you choose to keep Me in the center of your thoughts, you can live more peacefully. My Peace helps you stay calm in tough and stressful times. We can deal with your problems together—you and I—so there's no need to worry or fear.

I know that the more difficult your troubles are, the more you want to fix them yourself. Your thoughts wander *away* from Me and *to* your troubles. When this happens, say My Name. Shout it, whisper it, or just think it. Saying My Name will help you remember that I am with you, I am in control, and I will help.

Don't be worried by how often your mind wanders. Keeping Me in your thoughts is a new habit that will take time and practice. But the rewards are wonderful! The more your thoughts stay with Me, the more Peace and Joy you'll have in your life.

A child will be born to us. God will give a son to us. He will be responsible for leading the people. His name will be Wonderful Counselor, Powerful God, Father Who Lives Forever, Prince of Peace.

—Isaiah 9:6

I can do all things through Christ
because he gives me strength.

—Philippians 4:13

The name of the Lord is a strong tower;
the righteous run to it and are safe.

—Proverbs 18:10 nkjv

If God is
your partner,
make your
plans BIG!

—D. L. Moody

Be strong
and courageous,
all you who
put your hope
in the Lord!

—Psalm 31:24 nlt

Listening and Loving

I want you to *love Me*, listen to Me, and *stay close to Me*.

When you are close to someone, listening and loving are so very important. To really listen to someone shows that you care about that person. And when someone you love is speaking, you want to understand. So you listen carefully.

To be closer to Me, listen as I *sing about you with Joy and Love*. Ask the Holy Spirit to help you receive My Love more and more. Then a wonderful thing will happen: You will be able to love Me even more!

This world is full of dangers, so it is wise to stay close by My side. Listen to Me—listen to My Spirit when you pray and to My Word when you read. I will guide you through tough times. *Tell Me all your problems*, remembering that *I am your Protection*. I'll help you handle whatever troubles you face. *Stay close to Me*.

Love the Lord your God. Obey him. Stay close to him. He is your life. And he will let you live many years in the land. This is the land he promised to give your ancestors Abraham, Isaac and Jacob.

—Deuteronomy 30:20

The Lord your God is with you. The mighty One will save you. The Lord will be happy with you. You will rest in his love. He will sing and be joyful about you.

—Zephaniah 3:17

People, trust God all the time. Tell him all your problems. God is our protection.

—Psalm 62:8

Build Wisely

Like a house, your life must be built on a strong and sure foundation. Make *Me* that foundation. Be like the wise man who built his house on the rock. Build your life on Me. When the winds of life blow, you will not be shaken.

Don't try to build on popularity, the things you own, or even your own talents. These things won't last forever. Making them the foundation for your life would be like the foolish man building his house on sand. When the winds blow hard, a life built on unstable, temporary things will fall with a great crash.

Trying to live without Me is *"Useless! Useless!"* Remember—I never change or leave you. Yes, there will still be wind and storms, but I'll help you stand strong. The key is to *keep Me before you always*. Keep talking to Me. Step by step, I'll guide you. I'll show you the right way to live.

"Everyone who hears these things I say and obeys them is like a wise man. The wise man built his house on rock. It rained hard and the water rose. The winds blew and hit that house. But the house did not fall, because the house was built on rock."

—MATTHEW 7:24–27

The Teacher says, "Useless! Useless! Completely useless! All things are useless."

—ECCLESIASTES 1:2

He lifted me out of the pit of destruction, out of the sticky mud. He stood me on a rock. He made my feet steady.

—PSALM 40:2

I keep the Lord before me always. Because he is close by my side I will not be hurt.

—PSALM 16:8

Look the Right Way

You get to choose which direction you look and what you focus on. So look the right way!

In the world around you, there are beautiful things and ugly things. I created you to enjoy beauty and goodness; they are My gifts to you. When you look the right way—toward what is *true and right and beautiful*—you'll be encouraged and made stronger in your faith.

As you go through your day, you'll also encounter things that are wrong or ugly. You may have to deal with them, but you don't have to keep thinking about them. Choose to think about what is good instead—kind words, people who help others, God's beautiful creation. You can enjoy even the beauty of a tiny flower in the crack of a sidewalk. These blessings will help you remember that I am with you in your day. Listen to Me. Hear Me saying, "Look the *right* way."

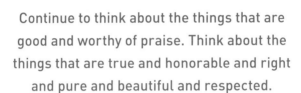

Continue to think about the things that are good and worthy of praise. Think about the things that are true and honorable and right and pure and beautiful and respected.

—Philippians 4:8

"My sheep listen to my voice. I know them, and they follow me."

—John 10:27

"May the Lord show you his kindness. May he have mercy on you."

—Numbers 6:25

You will teach me God's way to live. Being with you will fill me with joy. At your right hand I will find pleasure forever.

—Psalm 16:11

The Adventure

You are in training—like a great explorer preparing for the biggest adventure of your life. Trust Me to be your Guide.

I designed this adventure you're living. It is different from everyone else's. You didn't choose it, but it's the way I planned for you. You won't always understand the things I'm doing. That's why I say, "Trust Me!"

The struggles of this world can be like a jungle, thick and dark. You can't see what's around you or what's waiting for you in the shadows. So hold on to My hand as I guide you through the darkness. Follow *Me*. I will show you the safe path. Although you cannot see Me, you can trust that I am with you, taking care of you.

Don't focus on the problems in your life. Focus on *Me*. Put your hope in My Presence with you and My promises to help you. Then just wait and see all that I will do for you!

Trust in the Lᴏʀᴅ with all your heart, and do not lean on your own understanding.

—Pʀᴏᴠᴇʀʙs 3:5 ᴇsᴠ

Who among you fears the Lord and obeys his servant? That person may walk in the dark and have no light. Then let him trust in the Lord. Let him depend on his God.

—Isᴀɪᴀʜ 50:10

Why am I so sad? Why am I so upset? I should put my hope in God. I should keep praising him.

—Psᴀʟм 42:5

I will look to the Lord for help. I will wait for God to save me. My God will hear me.

—Mɪᴄᴀʜ 7:7

The Power of a Prayer

Everyone has worries and troubles. They're no fun, but you can use them for good. Use them to grow closer to Me.

Whenever a worry starts to worm its way into your mind, toss it out by talking to Me. Create your own collection of quick prayers, such as: *Help me, Jesus. I need Your Peace. Show me what to do.* These prayers are like vitamins for your soul—the more you say them, the stronger you will be.

When you use your troubles to grow closer to Me, you can actually be *happy* in spite of them. Of course, it takes practice to remember to pray instead of worry. That's why it's so important to have those quick prayers ready to use.

When you face problems of any kind, pray boldly. Your prayers are like poison to the devil. Pray, and he'll run away—but I'll stay right by your side.

Lord, teach me your ways. Guide me to do what is right because I have enemies.

—Psalm 27:11

You will have many kinds of troubles. But when these things happen, you should be very happy.

—James 1:2

So give yourselves to God. Stand against the devil, and the devil will run away from you. Come near to God, and God will come near to you. You are sinners. So clean sin out of your lives. You are trying to follow God and the world at the same time. Make your thinking pure.

—James 4:7–8

Lord, hear my prayer. Listen to my cry for mercy. Come to help me because you are loyal and good.

—Psalm 143:1

Lord of Peace

I am the Lord of Peace. I give you Peace *at all times and in every way.*

There is a hole inside every person that can only be filled by Me and My Peace. People who don't know Me try to fill that hole with other things—friends, sports, hobbies, their stuff, and sometimes bad things too. Other people simply pretend the hole isn't there. Even My children can forget that they need Me *at all times.*

But knowing you need Me is only half the battle. The other half is believing that I can—and will—*give you everything you need.*

My Peace is a gift to My followers; I paid for it on the cross. All you have to do to receive My gift is admit that you need it. Open your heart—and fill the hole inside you—by saying, "Jesus, I accept Your Peace."

We pray that the Lord of peace will give
you peace at all times and in every way.
May the Lord be with all of you.

—2 Thessalonians 3:16

My God will use his wonderful riches in Christ
Jesus to give you everything you need.

—Philippians 4:19

"I leave you peace. My peace I give you. I do not
give it to you as the world does. So don't let
your hearts be troubled. Don't be afraid."

—John 14:27

A Christian . . .
knows that hope
is a beam of God,
a spark of glory,
and that nothing
shall extinguish
it till the soul be
filled with glory.

—THOMAS BROOKS

Don't envy sinners.
But always
respect the Lord.
If you do, you
will have hope
for the future.
Your wishes will
come true.

—Proverbs 23:17–18

Put Me First

In everything you do, put Me first. *Remember Me, and I will give you success.*

Putting Me first sounds easy enough, but this world and the devil make it very hard to do. Other things—even good things—creep in to fill up your time. If this only happens once in a while, it's just part of being human. But if it happens a lot, watch out! You've stopped putting Me first. This isn't just another rule. It's the only way to live with lasting Joy—close to Me.

How can you make Me number one in your life? Talk to Me first thing in the morning. Decide when you will read My Word, and then do it. Sports, hobbies, and friends are good things. But don't let them take the place of time with Me. I want you to *enjoy* getting to know Me and *serving Me* first. And as you *live in My Light*—close to Me—*I will give you success.*

Remember the Lord in everything you
do. And he will give you success.
—Proverbs 3:6

"But I have this against you: You have left
the love you had in the beginning."
—Revelation 2:4

Enjoy serving the Lord. And he will
give you what you want.
—Psalm 37:4

God is in the light. We should live in the light,
too. If we live in the light, we share fellowship
with each other. And when we live in the
light, the blood of the death of Jesus, God's
Son, is making us clean from every sin.
—1 John 1:7

Trust Me

Trust Me every minute, every second. That's all I ask of you; I promise it will keep you strong.

Each day is a victory as long as you stay with Me. Look for Me in your day—I am here! Keeping your thoughts centered on Me is the best way to find Me. Write a verse on your mirror. Tuck a note in your notebook. Give yourself reminders of My Presence.

Even on hard days, I want you to trust Me. Pray and ask Me to help you and guide you one step at a time. Because I'm always near, I know *exactly* how hard things are for you and exactly what you need.

Though the battle is tough and you may feel weak, I am strong. Remember that My Holy Spirit—*your Helper*—is All-Powerful *and* loving and ready to help. Call out My Name, and *My Love will surround you.*

People, trust God all the time. Tell him all
your problems. God is our protection.
—Psalm 62:8

"I will ask the Father, and he will give you
another Helper. He will give you this Helper to
be with you forever. The Helper is the Spirit of
truth. The world cannot accept him because it
does not see him or know him. But you know
him. He lives with you and he will be in you."
—John 14:16–17

Wicked people have many troubles. But the
Lord's love surrounds those who trust him.
—Psalm 32:10

Too Many to Count

This world gives you so many things to worry about—too many to even count! Everywhere you look, there are problems and troubles. They're on the news, in your school, in your family, and sometimes even in your own life. Let Me comfort you.

Come to Me when you are tired and have a heavy load. In the middle of all the mess, let Me help you. Whisper My Name, *"Jesus!"* It will help you remember I'm with you, bigger than any worry or trouble in this world, to comfort you and bring you Joy.

Use worries as reminders to look for Me—for My Presence, My Peace, and My Love. I am with you at all times and in every place. When you look for Me, I will give you Joy that will never go away. And I will give you blessings—too many to even count!

I was very worried. But you comforted
me and made me happy.

—Psalm 94:19

"Now you are sad. But I will see you again and you
will be happy. And no one will take away your joy."

—John 16:22

"Come to me, all of you who are tired and have
heavy loads. I will give you rest. Accept my work
and learn from me. I am gentle and humble in
spirit. And you will find rest for your souls."

—Matthew 11:28–29

Sing to Me

In this world of phones and cameras and computers, it can be hard to get away. It can be difficult to find a safe, quiet place to rest—away from all the noise and distractions of this world. But remember this: *I am your Hiding Place.* Call out to Me, and I will *protect you.* I will *fill you with My songs.*

One of the best ways to reach out to Me is to sing praises to Me. The praises of My people are My throne. So when problems are weighing you down, break free by singing to Me—with music, with shouts, even in whispers. Your songs invite Me into your life, and I chase away the darkness. Troubles fade away as you praise and worship Me.

When you sing to Me, both you and I are blessed. I come near to you, and *I keep you safe in My shelter.*

Lord, save me from my enemies.
I come to you for safety.
—Psalm 143:9

You are my hiding place. You protect me from my
troubles. You fill me with songs of salvation.
—Psalm 32:7

You sit as the Holy One. The praises
of Israel are your throne.
—Psalm 22:3

You protect them by your presence from
what people plan against them. You keep
them safe in your shelter from evil words.
—Psalm 31:20

Enough

My grace is *enough* for you. It will get you through your toughest times.

It's easy to believe this when everything is good and going your way. It's much harder to believe it when nothing seems to be working out. But *that* is when My grace actually shines the brightest—when you know you need My help.

I want your life to be filled with *the very great riches of My grace*—My mercy, care, and kindness. My grace is My free gift to you. It gives you what you need to live right now, in this messy world. And it also gives you what you need to live in heaven one day with Me.

So tell Me all that you're thinking and feeling and hoping. I won't always say yes to what you ask, but I *will* always take care of you. And I listen, understand, and love you with all My heart, at all times. As you depend on Me, I give you more and more of My Power—and it will always be enough.

The Lord said to me, "My grace is enough for you. When you are weak, then my power is made perfect in you." So I am very happy to brag about my weaknesses. Then Christ's power can live in me.

—2 Corinthians 12:9

He raised us up with Christ and gave us a seat with him in the heavens. . . . He did this so that for all future time he could show the very great riches of his grace. He shows that grace by being kind to us in Christ Jesus.

—Ephesians 2:6–7

"The mountains may disappear, and the hills may come to an end. But my love will never disappear. My promise of peace will not come to an end."

—Isaiah 54:10

While You Wait

Keep your thoughts focused on Me! I am with you. I am taking care of you.

When you're hurting, it may not seem like I am taking care of you; but I am. It's just that sometimes I ask you to wait. And remember: There are many different ways to wait, and some are much better than others. My kind of waiting means always trusting and hoping in Me—even when you don't understand and even when things aren't going as you'd like.

Thank Me for the times that you need Me. They bring us closer together. Trust that I know what I'm doing—that I can bring good out of every trouble you ever face. Don't stop hoping, no matter what you've already been through. Believe that I am the Lord of your future and that I have good things planned for you. My plans will *give you hope and a good future.*

The Lord is good to those who put their hope in him. He is good to those who look to him for help.
—Lamentations 3:25

We know that in everything God works for the good of those who love him. They are the people God called, because that was his plan.
—Romans 8:28

"I say this because I know what I have planned for you," says the Lord. "I have good plans for you. I don't plan to hurt you. I plan to give you hope and a good future."
—Jeremiah 29:11

Satan trembles
when he
sees the
weakest saint
upon his knees.

—WILLIAM COWPER

Don't be
afraid of them.
The Lord
your God will
fight for you.

—Deuteronomy 3:22

Safe and Secure

Everyone wants to feel safe and secure. I know you want that too. Put your trust in Me, and I will look out for you. In fact, I am the only One who can keep you safe and secure for all time.

Whenever you start to feel unsure or unsafe—about *anything*—come to Me. First, tell Me your fears. Then, tell Me that you trust Me. Saying out loud that you trust Me brings Me even closer to you. And it also sends Satan—with all his lies and schemes—running away so that you are *free* from his evil ways.

Since the Garden of Eden, the devil has been telling lies. One of his biggest lies is that you don't need Me. Don't listen to Him! Put your trust in Me, because I am *the truth*, and I will keep you in my care.

Being afraid of people can get you into trouble.
But if you trust the Lord, you will be safe.

—Proverbs 29:25

Then the Lord God said to the woman,
"What have you done?"
She answered, "The snake tricked
me. So I ate the fruit."

—Genesis 3:13

Jesus answered, "I am the way. And I
am the truth and the life. The only way
to the Father is through me."

—John 14:6

"Then you will know the truth. And
the truth will make you free."

—John 8:32

Two Wonderful Truths

I am in control, and I am Good. These two wonderful truths tell you who I AM.

When you look at the world and all its troubles, it is sometimes hard to believe that both of these things can be true at the same time. Yes, I *am* in control of everything that happens. So when bad things take place, it can be hard to understand Me and trust that I am not some cruel, uncaring God.

But I *am* completely Good. *I am pure Light.* There is not one drop of darkness in Me.

Because you're human, you can never understand everything about Me. My ways and thoughts are too great and too different. When you're trying to make sense of why something has happened, come to Me. I may not explain, but I care about you, and I will listen. Trust Me to use bad things for good. *My ways*—even when you don't understand them— *are without fault.*

God will destroy death forever. The Lord God
will wipe away every tear from every face.
God will take away the shame of his people
from the earth. The Lord has spoken.

—Isaiah 25:8

Here is the message we have heard from
God and now tell to you: God is light, and
in him there is no darkness at all.

—1 John 1:5

The ways of God are without fault. The Lord's words
are pure. He is a shield to those who trust him.

—Psalm 18:30

Washed Away

Don't be afraid to tell Me the whole truth. Tell Me all your sins and mistakes. Don't try to run away or blame someone else. Instead, tell Me all that you have done.

Agree with Me that these things are wrong. Then leave them with Me. Be happy because I forgive you. I've already taken the punishment for all your sins.

When I forgive you, I *make you clean* again. But I don't just wash away your sins; I also cover you with My own goodness.

As you follow Me and *live in the Light* with Me, I am constantly washing away your sins. This lets you stay close to Me, in My Light. So celebrate—because you are forgiven. Be happy because you are washed clean. And *praise Me for My goodness*.

If we confess our sins, he will forgive our sins. We can trust God. He does what is right. He will make us clean from all the wrongs we have done.

—1 John 1:9

The Lord makes me very happy. All that I am rejoices in my God. The Lord has covered me with clothes of salvation. He has covered me with a coat of goodness. I am like a bridegroom dressed for his wedding. I am like a bride dressed in jewels.

—Isaiah 61:10

Happy are the people who know how to praise you. Lord, let them live in the light of your presence. In your name they rejoice all the time. They praise your goodness.

—Psalm 89:15–16

Putting the Puzzle Together

I am guiding you in wisdom. And I am leading you to do what is right. Some days it can be hard to figure out what the right thing is. On other days, you try to do the right thing, but it still turns out badly! It can all be very frustrating and . . . puzzling.

I want you to know that no matter what happens, I can bring something good out of every bit of it. This is My Wisdom. Trust Me, and I will lead you down the right path.

When you see something that is wrong or confusing, remember that you are seeing only one piece of the puzzle. I have the whole, finished puzzle in sight, and I know how each piece fits together perfectly. Trust Me to put all the pieces—even the ugly ones—into a beautiful and amazing picture for your life.

I am guiding you in wisdom. And I am
leading you to do what is right.

—Proverbs 4:11

We know that in everything God works for
the good of those who love him. They are the
people God called, because that was his plan.

—Romans 8:28

The Lord decides what a person does. So no
one can understand what his life is all about.

—Proverbs 20:24

Like Sunshine to a Flower

My Joy and Peace will feed your soul, just like the sunshine gives life to a flower. They will soak into you when you sit quietly with Me and trust Me.

The Joy of the Lord is My delightful gift to you. It *will make you strong*. My Joy is for all times—good and bad—though sometimes you may have to search for it. My Peace is also for all times. I give it to you when you trust in Me.

Remember that I am *the God who gives hope*. My Hope is not just wishful thinking; it is *knowing* for certain that I am your Savior and have reserved a home for you in heaven.

I bought this Hope for you on the cross. Because of this Hope, you can have Joy and Peace in Me right now. As they grow inside you, you will grow and bloom like a flower in the sunshine.

I pray that the God who gives hope will fill
you with much joy and peace while you
trust in him. Then your hope will overflow
by the power of the Holy Spirit.

—Romans 15:13

Nehemiah said [to all the people of Israel], . . .
"Today is a holy day to the Lord. Don't be sad.
The joy of the Lord will make you strong."

—Nehemiah 8:10

"There are many rooms in my Father's house.
I would not tell you this if it were not true. I
am going there to prepare a place for you.
After I go and prepare a place for you, I will
come back. Then I will take you to be with
me so that you may be where I am."

—John 14:2–3

My hope is not just
a wish for things to
be better; it is My
promise to you that
I will always help
you. I will carry your
troubles for you and
lighten your heart.
I am your ever-
present Help, so you
are never alone.

—*JESUS CALLING:*
365 DEVOTIONS FOR KIDS

As it is written in
the Scriptures:
"No one has ever
seen this.
No one has ever
heard about it.
No one has ever
imagined
what God has
prepared for those
who love him."

—1 CORINTHIANS 2:9

I Turn Darkness into Light

When you are going through a dark time—a hard time— it's easy to think that it will last forever. The longer you struggle, the darker it seems. You begin to imagine that good things will never happen again. You may even feel like giving up. That's why it's so very important to remember that *I* am always with you. And because I am in complete control, I can turn your darkness into Light.

When you feel like you just can't take any more, turn to Me for help. Hold on to Me so we can work through this hard time together. Don't focus on your problems. Instead, think about how I'm going to fix things for you. Then praise Me for My help that *is* coming.

As you walk by My side and look to Me in trust, My Light shines in your life. It will *grow brighter and brighter* until the dark times in your life shine like the day.

The Lord God has put his Spirit in me. This is because he has appointed me to tell the good news to the poor. He has sent me to comfort those whose hearts are broken.

—Isaiah 61:1

Lord, you give light to my lamp. The Lord brightens the darkness around me.

—2 Samuel 22:29

We live by what we believe, not by what we can see.

—2 Corinthians 5:7

The way of the good person is like the light of dawn. It grows brighter and brighter until it is full daylight.

—Proverbs 4:18

Only Peek at Your Problems

Gaze at Me and only peek at your problems. What does that mean? It means you should spend more time thinking about who I am and what I can do than you spend thinking about your problems. This is the secret of living with Joy.

It's natural to do the opposite: Gaze at your problems and only peek at Me. But I want you to live *super*naturally. And I have given you the power to do it. That's why I sent the Holy Spirit. The Spirit lives in everyone who follows Me. He will help you do what you cannot do for yourself.

Ask Him to warn you when you're thinking about your problems too much. Staying focused on Me is tough when the world and the devil want your attention! You need the Spirit's help. So ask Him to handle your problems while you gaze at Me. I am your forever Friend.

Let us look only to Jesus. He is the one who began our faith, and he makes our faith perfect. Jesus suffered death on the cross. But he accepted the shame of the cross as if it were nothing. He did this because of the joy that God put before him.

—Hebrews 12:2

"I will ask the Father, and he will give you another Helper. He will give you this Helper to be with you forever. The Helper is the Spirit of truth. The world cannot accept him because it does not see him or know him. But you know him. He lives with you and he will be in you."

—John 14:16–17

So we set our eyes not on what we see but on what we cannot see. What we see will last only a short time. But what we cannot see will last forever.

—2 Corinthians 4:18

Trust Me . . . Always

Trust in Me always. Trust Me because I am your Rock forever.

It's easy to trust Me for a while—especially when things are going well in your life. But I want you to trust Me always, no matter what is happening.

I know that's a difficult thing to ask, and I know that sometimes you'll mess it up. But I still love you perfectly, even then. And I still want you close to Me. When you make a mistake, tell Me—and let My Love pull you back to trusting Me.

You're not perfect, but I am. You won't always be sure of your next step, but I am *the Rock eternal*. I never change. You can always count on Me! I am solid; I will not break. I am strong enough to hold you up, as well as carry all your worries and burdens.

When you're feeling *tired* and loaded down, *lean on Me—trust Me with all your heart*. I won't ever let you down.

Trust the Lord always. Trust the Lord
because he is our Rock forever.
—Isaiah 26:4

"Come to me, all of you who are tired and
have heavy loads. I will give you rest."
—Matthew 11:28

Trust the Lord with all your heart. Don't
depend on your own understanding.
—Proverbs 3:5

The Joy of Hope

*B*e *joyful because you have hope.* It's not always easy to be joyful. Some days nothing goes right, and bad things happen all around you. How can you be happy on days like that? How can you find Joy? It can be found in My Hope.

My Hope promises that you are not alone, and that you have My help. This Hope that *I have chosen to give you* is *rich and glorious.* When you decide to follow Me, you become part of My royal family, and the blessings of My Hope are yours!

Like a hot-air balloon, My Hope will lift you above your troubles. It will help you to see how small they are when compared to My might and power. But to begin this amazing journey, you must first climb into the basket beneath the balloon. Trust My Hope to always hold you up—and to give you Joy.

Be joyful because you have hope. Be patient when trouble comes. Pray at all times.

—Romans 12:12

I always pray to the God of our Lord Jesus Christ—to the glorious Father. I pray that he will give you a spirit that will make you wise in the knowledge of God—the knowledge that he has shown you. I pray that you will have greater understanding in your heart. Then you will know the hope that God has chosen to give us. I pray that you will know that the blessings God has promised his holy people are rich and glorious.

—Ephesians 1:17–18

If you [respect the Lord], you will have hope for the future. Your wishes will come true.

—Proverbs 23:18

I Am Bigger

Even when you have trouble all around you, I will save you. So don't let troubles scare you. They may seem big, and you may feel small, but remember that I am *the Mighty One*, and I am *with you*. I am bigger and stronger than any problem in this world. *My Power will save you!*

Hold tightly to My hand—by talking to Me, by reading My Word, by praising Me. I will not only help you face your troubles, but you will grow stronger *because* you have faced them. There will be times when you feel tired and weak. Don't think this means I'm unhappy with you. It's simply part of living in this broken world. Remember that you are not alone. I am always with you.

Keep talking to Me. My Presence will *give you strength*, and I will *bless you with Peace*.

Lord, even when I have trouble all
around me, you will keep me alive.
When my enemies are angry, You will reach
down and save me by your power.

—Psalm 138:7

The Lord your God is with you. The mighty One will
save you. The Lord will be happy with you. You will
rest in his love. He will sing and be joyful about you.

—Zephaniah 3:17

Refuse to give in to the devil. Stand strong
in your faith. You know that your Christian
brothers and sisters all over the world are
having the same sufferings you have.

—1 Peter 5:9

The Lord gives strength to his people. The
Lord blesses his people with peace.

—Psalm 29:11

The Great Mystery

You are in Me, and I am in you. This is the great mystery of being a child of God.

I created everything in the universe, and I keep all things going. I tell the sun to rise and set. I keep the air filled with oxygen. I tell the plants and trees how to grow. I am Lord of all for all time.

It is by My Power that *you live and move and exist*. You are a human, but you are also My precious child. You and I live life *with* each other. But the amazing, wonderful mystery is that I also live *in* you. You are filled with *My Presence*.

I know everything about you—more than your best friend or your mom or dad. Every step you take, every word you speak, every breath you breathe—everything you do is in My Presence. And the more you are aware of Me, the more Joy you will feel. I will give meaning to *every* moment of your life.

"On that day you will know that I am in my Father. You will know that you are in me and I am in you."

—John 14:20

God decided to let his people know this rich and glorious truth which he has for all people. This truth is Christ himself, who is in you. He is our only hope for glory.

—Colossians 1:27

I pray that your life will be strong in love and be built on love. . . . Christ's love is greater than any person can ever know. But I pray that you will be able to know that love. Then you can be filled with the fullness of God.

—Ephesians 3:17, 19

"By his power we live and move and exist." Some of your own poets have said: "For we are his children."

—Acts 17:28

I Can Take Care of That

Give your worries to Me, and I will take care of you.

No matter what those worries are, I can—and will—carry you through them. Troubles with friends or family? I can take care of them. Troubles with school? I can take care of those too. Bad dreams, bad days, bad choices—I can handle *all* those things.

How? *Give them to Me* by telling Me about them. Then leave them with Me by not worrying about them anymore. Trust that I will work out everything in the way that's best for you.

You don't have to fix anything—that is what I am here for. Be patient and trust Me with all those things you can't control. My answer may take a little time, but I can—and will—take care of whatever is worrying you.

Give your worries to the Lord. He will take care
of you. He will never let good people down.
—PSALM 55:22

"Come to me, all you who are tired and have
heavy loads. I will give you rest. Accept my
work and learn from me. I am gentle and
humble in spirit. And you will find rest for your
souls. The work that I ask you to accept is easy.
The load I give you to carry is not heavy."
—MATTHEW 11:28–30

I trust in your love. My heart is
happy because you saved me.
—PSALM 13:5

I believe the Bible is the best gift God has ever given to man. All the good from the Savior of the world is communicated to us through this book.

—ABRAHAM LINCOLN

See how I love
your orders.
Lord, give me life
by your love.
Your words are true
from the start.
And all your laws
will be fair forever.

—Psalm 119:159–160

Tell Me All About It

Tough day? Hurt feelings? Confused? Take a deep breath and tell Me all about it. Wrap yourself up in My Love like a warm blanket. Let the Peace of My Presence and the strength of My Love soothe you.

Just take time to be with Me. Sit quietly and think about Me. Other thoughts—about what you want to do or what you should have said—will try to creep into your mind. Say *no* to them. Say *yes* to Me. Let My Peace fill your mind instead. My Peace *is so great that you cannot understand it*.

Yes, this world is full of trouble, but *I have defeated the world!* I will lift you above all its troubles. Simply say, "I trust You, Jesus. You are my Hope. I know that You will take care of me." Short, heartfelt prayers like this—prayers that you can say anytime and anywhere—will keep you close to Me.

Do not worry about anything. But pray and ask
God for everything you need. And when you pray,
always give thanks. And God's peace will keep your
hearts and minds in Christ Jesus. The peace that
God gives is so great that we cannot understand it.

—Philippians 4:6–7

"I told you these things so that you can have
peace in me. In this world you will have trouble.
But be brave! I have defeated the world!"

—John 16:33

[God] raised us up with Christ and gave us
a seat with him in the heavens. He did this
for those of us who are in Christ Jesus.

—Ephesians 2:6

Your Journey

Your life on earth is like a journey. It started the day you were born.

Sometimes your journey takes you through wonderful places and happy times. Other times, you travel up rocky mountains of trouble or through dark forests of fear. At every turn, around every corner, I am there, showing you the way. Your job is simply to *follow Me* wherever I lead.

It's true that sometimes I will lead you to a place you'd rather not go. I may ask you to do things you don't want to do—like move to a new school, be kind when others aren't, or listen to Me when no one else seems to. Yes, it will be hard. And you won't always understand My reasons. But trust Me. I use the tough times of your journey to bring you closer to Me, step after step. *I will brighten the darkness around you.*

Then Jesus said to Peter, "Follow me!"
—John 21:19

The Lord is my shepherd. I have everything I
need. . . . Even if I walk through a very dark valley,
I will not be afraid because you are with me. Your
rod and your shepherd's staff comfort me.
—Psalm 23:1, 4

Lord, you give light to my lamp. My God
brightens the darkness around me.
—Psalm 18:28

Let Me Fight for You

I will fight for you. You just have to stay calm.

You think you have to fix that problem all by yourself. You think you have to make peace in that friendship, straighten out that fuss with your parents, calm those hurt feelings all by yourself. But it isn't working very well, is it?

Stop struggling. Stop fighting your way through trouble. Let *Me fight for you*.

I know that's not easy to do. But you can trust that I am working in your life to make everything better. *Be still, and know that I am God*.

Keeping your body still can be tough. You want to run, jump, wiggle, and fidget. So keeping your mind and thoughts still can seem downright impossible! That's why I sent My Holy Spirit. Ask Him to calm your thoughts. Ask Him to show you how I'm working in your life. He will help you trust Me as I fight for you.

You will only need to remain calm.
The Lord will fight for you.

—Exodus 14:14

God says, "Be still and know that I am
God. I will be praised in all the nations. I
will be praised throughout the earth."

—Psalm 46:10

If a person's thinking is controlled by his sinful
self, then there is death. But if his thinking is
controlled by the Spirit, then there is life and peace.

—Romans 8:6

Those who go to God Most High for safety
will be protected by God All-Powerful.

—Psalm 91:1

I Am with You Always

I am with you—now and forever. But even though you know that *I will be with you always*, there may be times when you feel far away from Me. When those times come, simply pray, "Jesus, help me remember that You are here."

I created everything in this world, in the whole universe. I dotted the sky with stars. I set the moon and sun in their places. I carved out oceans and built up mountains. Every animal, every tree, every blade of grass is here because I created it.

Just look at the world around you, and see how great and powerful I am. There is nothing that can stop Me from keeping My promises to you. Let My Power amaze you, fill you with hope—and remind you that I am with you *always*.

Why am I so sad? Why am I so upset? I should put my hope in God. I should keep praising him, My Savior and my God.

—Psalm 42:5–6

"Go and make followers of all people in the world. Baptize them in the name of the Father and the Son and the Holy Spirit. Teach them to obey everything that I have told you. You can be sure that I will be with you always. I will continue with you until the end of the world."

—Matthew 28:19–20

You want things, but you do not have them. . . . You do not get what you want because you do not ask God.

—James 4:2

Seasons

The earth has seasons—summer and spring, winter and fall. Your life has seasons too, though they are harder to predict. Seasons of joy and happiness, of sorrow and sadness. *There is a right time for everything. Everything on earth has its special season*—even sadness.

When the season of sadness comes your way, don't be discouraged; it will not last forever. And I will always—in some way—use it for your good.

When you are hurting, look for signs of My Presence. I am there in the hug of your mom or dad, in the listening ear of a friend, in the rainbow I place in the sky. Look up to Me and see that My great Love is always shining on you. My Love and mercy never run out. *They are new every morning.*

Although the Lord brings sorrow, he
also has mercy. His love is great.
—LAMENTATIONS 3:32

There is a right time for everything. Everything
on earth has its special season.
—ECCLESIASTES 3:1

May the Lord show you his kindness.
May he have mercy on you.
—NUMBERS 6:25

The Lord's love never ends. His mercies never
stop. They are new every morning. Lord,
your loyalty is great. I say to myself, "The
Lord is what I have left. So I have hope."
—LAMENTATIONS 3:22–24

I Am Mighty!

I am *with you*, and I am *mighty*! Just as the sun is at the center of the solar system, so I am at the center of you—your body, your feelings, your thoughts, your soul. I, *the Mighty One* who created the universe, live *inside* you!

Just think: The Power of the One who made the earth and everything in it lives inside you! What does that mean? It means that you never have to worry about being weak. In fact, when you feel weak, *My Power is made perfect in you*. That is when I make you strongest.

Keep telling yourself that I live inside you, and I am mighty! Let My Presence chase away every doubt, every worry, every fear—and let it fill you *with great Joy*. My Power is always working in your life. I am making you *divinely* strong!

"The Lord your God is with you. The mighty
One will save you. The Lord will be happy
with you. You will rest in his love. He
will sing and be joyful about you."

—Zephaniah 3:17

But the Lord said to me, "My grace is enough for
you. When you are weak, then my power is made
perfect in you." So I am very happy to brag about my
weaknesses. Then Christ's power can live in me.

—2 Corinthians 12:9

God is strong and can help you not to fall.
He can bring you before his glory without
any wrong in you and give you great joy.

—Jude v. 24

Oh how sweet
to work for
God all day,
and then
lie down
at night
beneath
His smile.

—ROBERT MURRAY M'CHEYNE

"He will wipe away every tear from their eyes. There will be no more death, sadness, crying, or pain. All the old ways are gone." The One who was sitting on the throne said, "Look! I am making everything new!"

—Revelation 21:4–5

A Crown for You

I have a crown for you. It's better than any crown of silver or gold, better than any jewel. It is a crown of Love and mercy.

You depend on the blessings of Love and mercy, and giving them to you delights Me. To receive them, all you have to do is admit how much you need Me.

Many people don't want to confess this. They doubt anyone could ever give them all that they must have to live. And it's true—no *person* ever could. But I am God! There is no limit to what I can do for My children.

My Love is a gift. I give you *a love that will last forever*, and I give you tender mercy, again and again. I know you'll make mistakes. But I will forgive you when you come to Me. You are Mine, a royal child of the King. I bought you with My own blood. And I crown you with My Love and mercy.

All that I am, praise the Lord. Everything in me, praise his holy name. My whole being, praise the Lord. Do not forget all his kindnesses. The Lord forgives me for all my sins. He heals all my diseases. He saves my life from the grave. He loads me with love and mercy.

—Psalm 103:1–4

And from far away the Lord appeared to his people. He said, "I love you people with a love that will last forever. I became your friend because of my love and kindness."

—Jeremiah 31:3

Trust God all the time. Tell him all your problems. God is our protection.

—Psalm 62:8

You Are Mine

You belong to Me. I chose you and *called you out of darkness into My wonderful Light*.

Your connection to Me will protect you from feeling alone or lost in this ever-changing world. This means you don't have to rely on hurtful people or harmful things—I am the One who will *never* leave you. I chose you *before the world was made* and rescued you from the darkness of sin. You are a part of My royal family—forever!

Because you are Mine, I want you to share Me with others. I want you to *tell about all the wonderful things I have done*. This is how you can both serve Me and thank Me.

Telling others about Me is a great honor *and* a great responsibility. To do it, you need to know who I am. You can know Me by studying My Word. As we grow closer and closer, the Joy of My Presence will shine through you—and then others can see that you really do belong to Me!

You are a chosen people. You are the King's priests. You are a holy nation. You are a nation that belongs to God alone. God chose you to tell about the wonderful things he has done. He called you out of darkness into his wonderful light.

—1 Peter 2:9

Praise be to the God and Father of our Lord Jesus Christ. In Christ, God has given us every spiritual blessing in heaven. In Christ, he chose us before the world was made. In his love he chose us to be his holy people—people without blame before him.

—Ephesians 1:3–4

Enjoy serving the Lord. And he will give you what you want.

—Psalm 37:4

Be Brave!

Be strong and brave. Don't be afraid. I will be with you everywhere you go.

Did you know that you can be strong and brave even when you are feeling very weak? You can! The secret is in where you look. If you look only at yourself and the size of your problems, your courage will melt away like ice on a summer day. But if you look to Me and remember that I'm always *with* you and *for* you, you won't be afraid.

When things seem to be going wrong, don't get discouraged. Remember that I am a God of surprises: There is no limit to what I can do or how I can do it. I am creative and All-Powerful. *For Me all things are possible!*

Sometimes I'll answer your prayers right away. Other times, you'll have to wait. But I will always answer. *I am good to those who put their hope in Me. I am good to those who look to Me for help.*

"Remember that I commanded you to be strong and brave. So don't be afraid. The Lord your God will be with you everywhere you go."
—Joshua 1:9

Jesus looked at them and said, "For men this is impossible. But for God all things are possible."
—Matthew 19:26

The Lord is good to those who put their hope in him. He is good to those who look to him for help. It is good to wait quietly for the Lord to save.
—Lamentations 3:25–26

My Mighty Hand

*B*e *humble under My mighty hand.* This means I want you to trust My work—the work of My hand—in your life. Sometimes you can see that I am busy doing things for you, helping you; other times, it's not as obvious. But I am always with you, always working for good.

When you don't see Me, when you don't think I'm helping you, it's tempting to lose patience with My way of doing things. You want everything to change—*right now*! You might even get mad at Me. This will only make you feel worse.

Stop looking at that thing you want to change, and look at *Me* instead. Be brave enough to pray, "Lord, I humble myself under Your mighty hand. I will trust Your way, even though I don't understand it." This simple prayer will keep you from struggling against Me. And it will help you remember that I'm in control.

Trust My mighty hand to *lift you up.* I will take care of the thing that's troubling you—at just the *right time.*

So be humble under God's powerful hand. Then he will lift you up when the right time comes.

—1 Peter 5:6

The Lord has told you what is good. He has told you what he wants from you: Do what is right to other people. Love being kind to others. And live humbly, trusting your God.

—Micah 6:8

God gives us even more grace, as the Scripture says, "God is against the proud, but he gives grace to the humble." . . . Humble yourself before the Lord, and he will honor you.

—James 4:6, 10

Even on Bad Days

You've already figured out that life won't always go your way. Some days are tough, and not-so-good things happen. But you can *still* be happy. You can learn to find good even in the middle of not-so-good. Ask Me to show it to you.

Because you love and follow Me, *the devil is your enemy*. Every day he will try to trick you, telling you that right is wrong and wrong is right. *Be careful!* Use your *shield of faith. With that you can stop all the burning arrows of the Evil One.* The devil will whisper that you aren't really Mine. That is a lie! He will also tell you that there's no joy to be found in a bad day. Another lie!

This is the Truth: you belong to Me, I love you, and I can give you happiness even on bad days.

"Be still and know that I am God. I will be praised in all the nations. I will be praised throughout the earth."

—Psalm 46:10

"May the Lord show you his kindness. May he have mercy on you."

—Numbers 6:25

Control yourselves and be careful! The devil is your enemy. And he goes around like a roaring lion looking for someone to eat.

—1 Peter 5:8

Use the shield of faith. With that you can stop all the burning arrows of the Evil One.

—Ephesians 6:16

It Is I

When you don't know what to do, when you're worried or scared, stop and listen to Me. Hear Me saying, *"Have courage! It is I. Don't be afraid."*

Stress causes your thoughts to zoom around and around like race cars on a track. They roar so fast and loud that it's hard to hear My *quiet, gentle voice*. Ask the Holy Spirit to calm your mind so you can hear Me.

Remember, I am the *Prince of Peace*, and I am with you all the time. I am also in control of everything that happens to you. There is *nothing* that you and I can't handle together. And while I don't create bad things, I can turn them around and use them for good. This is how I heal the hurts you go through.

If your mind is racing, listen. I say to you, *"Have courage. It is I."* Search for Me in your day; watch for Me even in your troubles. Because *when you search for Me with all your heart, you will find Me!*

Jesus quickly spoke to them. He said,
"Have courage! It is I! Don't be afraid."
—Matthew 14:27

After the earthquake, there was a fire.
But the Lord was not in the fire. After the
fire, there was a quiet, gentle voice.
—1 Kings 19:12

A child will be born to us. God will give a son to
us. He will be responsible for leading the people.
His name will be Wonderful Counselor, Powerful
God, Father Who Lives Forever, Prince of Peace.
—Isaiah 9:6

"You will search for me. And when you search
for me with all your heart, you will find me!"
—Jeremiah 29:13

Hope is faith
holding out
its hand in
the dark.

—George Iles

My God brightens the darkness around me.

—Psalm 18:28

You'll Never Lose Me

Even though I give you countless good gifts, be careful of feeling like I owe them to you. When I give you good things, thank Me for them. But be ready to sometimes give them back to Me.

When you have lost something special (a friend, a toy, a place on a team), the last thing you expect to feel is Joy. It's okay to be sad, and it's okay to be upset. But, with time, I want you to remember all the good things you still have. Most of all, I want you to remember that you still have *Me*. Take Joy in knowing that I *will never leave you*.

This isn't how the world thinks, but God's children understand: Yes, you can *be sad* and still be *always rejoicing*—at the same time. The apostle Paul learned the secret of this. He was beaten, thrown in prison, and even shipwrecked! Yet the Holy Spirit helped Paul find Joy even in his hardest times. The secret is *Me*. Because no matter what you might lose, you'll never lose Me.

Be strong and brave. Don't be afraid of them.
Don't be frightened. The Lord your God will go
with you. He will not leave you or forget you.

—Deuteronomy 31:6

In every way we show that we are servants
of God. . . . We have much sadness, but we
are always rejoicing. We are poor, but we are
making many people rich in faith. We have
nothing, but really we have everything.

—2 Corinthians 6:4, 10

But I am always with you. You have held
my hand. You guide me with your advice.
And later you will receive me in honor.

—Psalm 73:23–24

Rest and Hope

Rest and hope go together—like macaroni and cheese, cookies and milk, you and Me.

As they try to find rest, some children search for the most comfortable bed, the softest pillow, or the most huggable bear. But you will really only *find rest in Me*. Not the sleeping kind of rest, but rather, rest—or relief—from worry and fear.

And *only I give you hope*. My kind of hope makes all the difference. For Paul and Silas, hope turned a prison cell into a concert of praise (Acts 16:25). For the man with leprosy, hope turned his homelessness into a homecoming (Luke 5:12–16). And hope can turn your impossible into possible—if you trust Me.

Your life is constantly changing, but I never change. I am *the same yesterday, today, and forever*. Because I love you with a perfect Love, I will give you the rest and hope you need.

I find rest in God; only he gives me hope.
He is my rock and my salvation. He is
my defender; I will not be defeated.

—Psalm 62:5–6 NCV

Moses said this about the people of Benjamin:
"The Lord's loved ones will lie down in
safety. The Lord protects them all day long.
The ones the Lord loves rest with him."

—Deuteronomy 33:12

Jesus Christ is the same yesterday,
today, and forever.

—Hebrews 13:8

Lord, show your love to us as
we put our hope in you.

—Psalm 33:22

More than Anything

I am always watching over you. No matter what you're doing, what you're going through, or how alone you may feel at times, I am with you—because I love you.

When you're hurting, it's easy to feel all alone. That's why it is so important that you remind yourself of this truth: *Nothing* can separate you from Me—no trouble, no fear, no mistake. Nothing, *absolutely nothing*, can separate you from My Love.

When times are tough, *trust Me. Don't depend on your own understanding*—lean on Me. I will hold you up, just as leaning on a rock helps you keep standing when you are tired. In fact, I am *the Rock of your protection*. Be happy, because the One who holds you up and protects you also loves you tenderly.

Yes, I am sure that nothing can separate us from
the love God has for us. Not death, not life, not
angels, not ruling spirits, nothing now, nothing
in the future, no powers, nothing above us,
nothing below us, or anything else in the whole
world will ever be able to separate us from the
love of God that is in Christ Jesus our Lord.

—Romans 8:38–39

Trust the Lord with all your heart. Don't
depend on your own understanding.

—Proverbs 3:5

But the Lord protects me like a strong, walled
city. My God is the rock of my protection.

—Psalm 94:22

Peace and Thankfulness

I want your life to be filled with Peace and thankfulness. These two things are closely connected. The more thankful you are, the more you'll be able to feel My Peace. And the more peaceful you are, the more thankful you'll be.

Being quiet and calm helps you see the many, many blessings I shower upon you every day. This calm thankfulness comes from your confidence that I do what's best—every single time. Even when things don't make sense.

If you start to feel worried or nervous or upset, let those feelings remind you to talk to Me. Take time to tell Me what's bothering you. Bring Me all your needs—big and small. I'll give you a Peace *so great that you cannot understand it*.

Because you belong to Me, I'll guard your heart and mind with My Peace. *Let My Peace control your thinking—and always be thankful.*

Let the peace that Christ gives control your thinking. You were all called together in one body to have peace. Always be thankful.

—Colossians 3:15

The ways of God are without fault. The Lord's words are pure. He is a shield to those who trust him.

—Psalm 18:30

Do not worry about anything. But pray and ask God for everything you need. And when you pray, always give thanks. And God's peace will keep your hearts and minds in Christ Jesus. The peace that God gives is so great that we cannot understand it.

—Philippians 4:6–7

The Devil and His Tricks

Whenever you look for Me, you will find Me. I am *with you always*. That's My promise to everyone who trusts Me as Savior. But to be blessed by this promise, you must look for Me. That sounds simple, but the devil will try to stop you.

The devil has three weapons: distractions, lies, and discouragement.

First, he likes to distract you. He'll show you the world and all its sparkles, so that you won't think about Me. Want to send the devil running? Just smile and whisper My Name. The devil also lies, just as he did to Adam and Eve. But you can know the truth—just read My Word. And the devil tries to discourage you, making you feel all alone and without hope. Just keep this in mind: You are never alone. I am with you every moment of every day.

Stand up to the devil and his tricks. When you do, he'll run, and *you'll find Me.*

The Lord will stay with you as long as you stay with him! Whenever you look for him, you will find him. But if you forsake him, he will forsake you.

—2 Chronicles 15:2 tlb

"So go and make followers of all people in the world. Baptize them in the name of the Father and the Son and the Holy Spirit. Teach them to obey everything that I have told you. You can be sure that I will be with you always. I will continue with you until the end of the world."

—Matthew 28:19–20

Then the Lord God said to the woman,
"What have you done?"
She answered, "The snake tricked
me. So I ate the fruit."

—Genesis 3:13

Your Anchor

An anchor holds a ship in a safe place, even when storms come. My Hope is *an anchor for your soul*—it holds you *sure and strong* in a safe place with Me.

In stormy weather, a large ship may not be able to get to safety because of the wild waves. So a smaller boat will carry the ship's anchor through the rough waters and into the harbor. The anchor is dropped in the harbor and the large ship is safe, even though it's still in stormy seas.

This is a picture of how My Hope keeps your soul—the part of you that lives forever—secure in the middle of life's storms.

I died to pay for your sins. After I died, I was raised to life again. My resurrection made Me your *living Hope*. When you anchor your life to Me, I'll keep you safe and sure—even in life's worst storms.

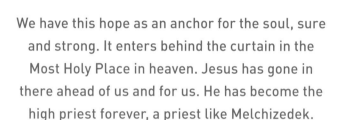

We have this hope as an anchor for the soul, sure and strong. It enters behind the curtain in the Most Holy Place in heaven. Jesus has gone in there ahead of us and for us. He has become the high priest forever, a priest like Melchizedek.

—HEBREWS 6:19–20

Praise be to the God and Father of our Lord Jesus Christ. God has great mercy, and because of his mercy he gave us a new life. He gave us a living hope because Jesus Christ rose from death.

—1 PETER 1:3

Let us hold firmly to the hope that
we have confessed. We can trust
God to do what he promised.

—HEBREWS 10:23

God delights
to increase
the faith of
His children.

—GEORGE MUELLER

Why am I so sad?
Why am I so upset?
I should put my
hope in God.
I should keep
praising him,
My Savior and
my God.

—Psalm 42:5–6

The Truth

I came into your life to *make you free*. The closer you live to Me, the freer you will be. Spend time alone with Me. Talk to Me. Listen to Me. Study My Word. As you do, you'll begin to see Me everywhere in your life. Your faith in Me will grow deeper and stronger.

You'll also see more and more of My Goodness. It will warm your heart like the sunshine warms your face. And My Goodness will help you see the people and things around you in a new way. You'll see them as *I* see them.

By spending time with Me, you'll come to know the Truth—about who I am and all I've done for you. You will learn the truth about yourself too—about who you are and all you can be with Me in your life. *You will know the truth. And the truth will make you free.*

"You will know the truth. And the
truth will make you free."

—John 8:32

How great is your goodness! You have stored it up for
those who fear you. You do good things for those who
trust you. You do this for all to see. You protect them
by your presence from what people plan against them.
You keep them safe in your shelter from evil words.

—Psalm 31:19–20

"But for you who honor me, goodness will shine on
you like the sun. There will be healing in its rays. You
will jump around, like calves freed from their stalls."

—Malachi 4:2

Now, those who are in Christ Jesus are not judged
guilty. I am not judged guilty because in Christ Jesus
the law of the Spirit that brings life made me free. It
made me free from the law that brings sin and death.

—Romans 8:1–2

A Happy Heart

A happy heart is like good medicine. And you have every reason to be happy, because *I have defeated the world.* With My death on the cross, I have completely conquered every power on this earth—and beyond! No one has any power to harm you.

Nothing in this *whole world will ever be able to separate you from My Love.* As you think about the wonderful things I have done for you, let happiness fill your heart. Let it shine from your face.

When you feel sick—sick at heart or sick in your body— a happy, thankful heart will help you feel better. So start thinking of all the things you have to be thankful for. Take time to praise Me for who I am and for all I've done for you. Let Me fill you with My Light and Life. Be happy because you are Mine!

A happy heart is like good medicine. But a broken spirit drains your strength.

—Proverbs 17:22

"I told you these things so that you can have peace in me. In this world you will have trouble. But be brave! I have defeated the world!"

—John 16:33

Nothing above us, nothing below us, or anything else in the whole world will ever be able to separate us from the love of God that is in Christ Jesus our Lord.

—Romans 8:39

My Love Goes on Forever

I am Good and *My Love goes on forever*. So thank Me! Praise Me!

My perfect Goodness means that I'll *always* do what is best for you. If there were even a speck of badness in Me, you would be in big trouble! You may not understand everything that happens, but I promise to use *everything* that happens for your good.

It takes great faith to trust Me when you see some of the sad and terrible things that happen in this world. But *you must live by what you believe* about Me, *not by what you can see* in the world.

One of the best ways to strengthen your belief is to praise Me. Praise takes your thoughts away from the things of this world, and it puts them on the wonderful Treasure you have in Me. *The praises of My people are My throne.* The more you praise Me, the closer you'll be to Me. Remember: *My Love continues forever!*

Come into his city with songs of thanksgiving.
Come into his courtyards with songs of
praise. Thank him, and praise his name. The
Lord is good. His love continues forever.
His loyalty continues from now on.

—Psalm 100:4–5

We live by what we believe, not by what we can see.

—2 Corinthians 5:7

You sit as the Holy One. The praises
of Israel are your throne.

—Psalm 22:3

Give thanks to the Lord because he is good. His
love continues forever. Give thanks to the God over
all gods. His love continues forever. Give thanks to
the Lord of all lords. His love continues forever.

—Psalm 136:1–3

Worth Bragging About

It's tempting to point to yourself and what you've done: You made the team; you made the cast of the play; you made the highest grade. But remember, anything you do is because of the gifts *I* give you.

If you want to brag, brag that you understand and know Me. Brag that I am the Lord. This is really the only thing worth boasting about.

So how can you *know* Me? Talk to Me all throughout your day. Just a few words can keep you thinking about Me. Learn about who I am by reading the Bible. Memorize My words so that you'll always have them with you. And see Me—see My glory in the beauty of nature all around you.

This world moves fast and so many things demand your time—school, church, family and friends, the Internet and TV, chores and hobbies. Put getting to know Me *first*. There's nothing more important. There's nothing else worth bragging about.

"But if someone wants to brag, let him brag about this: Let him brag that he understands and knows me. Let him brag that I am the Lord. Let him brag that I am kind and fair. Let him brag that I do things that are right on earth. This kind of bragging pleases me," says the Lord.

—Jeremiah 9:24

The heavens tell the glory of God. And the skies announce what his hands have made. Day after day they tell the story. Night after night they tell it again.

—Psalm 19:1–2

Jesus answered, "'Love the Lord your God with all your heart, soul and mind.' This is the first and most important command."

—Matthew 22:37–38

Like Air for Your Soul

Air. You breathe it in and out, every moment of every day. You *must* have it. I want to be like air for your heart and soul. I want you to think of Me and trust Me with each breath you take.

Practice being in My Presence. Your thoughts can easily wander away from Me, but it's also easy to bring them back where they belong. Simply say My Name—"Jesus"—and I am right there with you. Whisper it, sing it, shout it, or think it. My Name means "The Lord saves." Trust Me. Follow Me, and I will save you.

Say My Name and add words of love and praise to it. Let your heart pour out thanks for all that I am and for all that I do for you. Trust in My Love—it is yours *forever and ever.* Breathe it in like air for your soul.

I wait patiently for God to save me. Only he gives me hope. He is my rock, who saves me. He protects me like a strong, walled city. I will not be defeated.

—Psalm 62:5–6

But I am like an olive tree growing in God's temple. I trust God's love forever and ever.

—Psalm 52:8

She will give birth to a son. You will name the son Jesus. Give him that name because he will save his people from their sins.

—Matthew 1:21

Every Reason to Be Happy

Be happy! Shout with joy! You have every reason to be happy, because I am here with you *now*, and because heaven is waiting for you *in the future*.

I have already paid for your sins and mistakes. I have covered you with My own perfection. This is My Gift to all those who call Me Savior. No matter what's going on in your life, you can count on Me. No one will be able to *steal you out of My hand*. In Me, you have complete safety forever!

Pray at all times, especially when you are struggling. That's when you need to talk to Me the most, though it may be harder to find the words. Ask the Holy Spirit to *control your thinking* and help you pray. Your prayers don't have to be pretty or perfect; just pour out your heart to Me. Then trust Me—you have every reason to *have hope* and *be patient* in the midst of trouble.

Be joyful because you have hope. Be patient
when trouble comes. Pray at all times.
—Romans 12:12

God's grace has come. That grace can save every
person. . . . [Our great God and Savior Jesus Christ]
is our great hope, and he will come with glory.
—Titus 2:11, 13

"I give [my followers] eternal life, and
they will never die. And no person
can steal them out of my hand."
—John 10:28

If a person's thinking is controlled by his sinful
self, then there is death. But if his thinking is
controlled by the Spirit, then there is life and peace.
—Romans 8:6

Faith expects
from God
what is
beyond all
expectation.

—Andrew Murray

Put your
hope in
the Lord
because he
is loving
and able
to save.

—Psalm 130:7

The Secret of Being Happy

I want you to learn *the secret of being happy*—untroubled, at peace, still able to trust Me—not just when everything is going great, but anytime. When you stub your toe, get cut from the team, or get grounded. When your feelings are hurt or your nose is stuffy. Even when the worst thing you can imagine happens. No, you may not be the birthday-party kind of happy. But you can be happy knowing that I love you and will take care of you.

Putting this secret into practice takes work. First, tell Me everything—*all your problems*, all your joys. Nothing is too big or small. I'll listen to your every word, and I will understand. Also, read and reread Bible verses that help you. Finally, praise Me because you know I'm already working on the answer for you.

Praise Me because it will make you feel better. And praise Me because *it is good to tell of My love*. This is the secret of being truly happy.

I know how to live when I am poor. And I know how to live when I have plenty. I have learned the secret of being happy at any time in everything that happens. I have learned to be happy when I have enough to eat and when I do not have enough to eat. I have learned to be happy when I have all that I need and when I do not have the things I need.

—Philippians 4:12

People, trust God all the time. Tell him all your problems. God is our protection.

—Psalm 62:8

It is good to praise the Lord, to sing praises to God Most High. It is good to tell of your love in the morning and of your loyalty at night.

—Psalm 92:1–2

In Training

Like an athlete, you are in training. Not to run a four-minute mile or to swim in the Olympics, but to climb the mountain of life. It's a long journey, and it can sometimes be hard to keep going and keep trying to do the right thing. But I'm training you to take one step after another, even when it's tough. *Look at Me and My example so that you will not get tired and stop trying.*

You live in a world that wants only easy and fun. So when hard times come, it can be tempting to feel sorry for yourself. Don't do that! Choose to see your struggles as a chance to learn more about Me and My ways, to grow closer to Me.

Struggles help you remember that you need Me—they make heaven even more precious and real to you. Turn to Me and whisper My Name, trusting Me to take care of You. When you do, I wrap you up in My forever Love.

Think about Jesus. He held on patiently while sinful men were doing evil things against him. Look at Jesus' example so that you will not get tired and stop trying.

—Hebrews 12:3

Our homeland is in heaven, and we are waiting for our Savior, the Lord Jesus Christ, to come from heaven. He will change our humble bodies and make them like his own glorious body. Christ can do this by his power. With that power he is able to rule all things.

—Philippians 3:20–21

The Lord appeared to his people. He said, "I love you people with a love that will last forever. I became your friend because of my love and kindness."

—Jeremiah 31:3

Strong Again

When you're in the middle of a tough time, your mind races. You start thinking through every possible answer. You practice what you will say and what you will do. You wonder what you can take care of yourself and who you can call on for help. And if you don't see the answer to your problem right away, you start to worry.

Stop! *If you will be calm and trust Me, you will be strong.*

Take a deep breath and be quiet. Make time to talk to Me. Trust Me and My ways even though you aren't sure what to do. Trying to fix everything on your own will only lead to more worry. Choosing to trust will give you peace and strength. *I will not leave you* when you need Me.

Keep telling Me all about your worries and troubles, and keep waiting for My help. It may not come right away, but it will come. I promise. And you *will become strong again*.

This is what the Lord God, the Holy One of Israel, says: "If you come back to me and trust me, you will be saved. If you will be calm and trust me, you will be strong." But you don't want to do that.

—Isaiah 30:15

Be strong and brave. Don't be afraid of them. Don't be frightened. The Lord your God will go with you. He will not leave you or forget you.

—Deuteronomy 31:6

The people who trust the Lord will become strong again. They will be able to rise up as an eagle in the sky. They will run without needing rest. They will walk without becoming tired.

—Isaiah 40:31

I Will Never Fail You

Put your hope in My Love. It never fails.

In this world, failure is all around you—people make mistakes, friends lie, and even family can sometimes let you down. And you? You make plenty of mistakes and bad choices too. So the idea of a Love that never fails can be hard to understand—but it is yours to have. And it is only found in Me.

I am God, perfect and forever. Yet I came down to earth as a tiny baby. I grew up here on earth. I was once exactly your age. I know everything you're going through: struggles with schoolwork, with fitting in, even with family. I understand, and *My mercies never stop.*

Hope in Me and in My amazing gift—*salvation and goodness that will never end.* Choose to trust Me. *I am pleased with those who trust My Love*—and I will never let you down.

The Lord is pleased with those who fear
him, with those who trust his love.

—Psalm 147:11

The Lord's love never ends. His mercies never stop.

—Lamentations 3:22

We know the love that God has for us, and
we trust that love. God is love. Whoever lives
in love lives in God, and God lives in him.

—1 John 4:16

"Look up to the heavens. Look around you
at the earth below. The skies will disappear
like clouds of smoke. The earth will become
useless like old clothes. Its people will die
like flies. But my salvation will continue
forever. My goodness will never end."

—Isaiah 51:6

I Am Holy

Holy, holy, holy is the Lord God All-Powerful. Three times I am called *holy*. There is absolutely no sin in Me.

Yes, I am always with you, but don't forget that I am also completely holy. Remembering that will help you understand how very blessed you are to be able to call Me your Savior and Friend. And it will help you be careful with My Name.

When you say My Name, remember you are talking to *Me*. Don't use My Name improperly or without thinking, the way the world does.

I know there will be times when you forget My holiness, when you are careless with My Name. Even King David, who was *a man after My own heart*, made mistakes. When he saw his mistakes, he hurried to Me to say, *"I have sinned against the Lord."* So don't be afraid when you realize you have sinned. Instead, hurry to Me. Ask Me to forgive you—and I will.

Each of these four living things had six wings. The living things were covered all over with eyes, inside and out. Day and night they never stop saying: "Holy, holy, holy is the Lord God All-Powerful. He was, he is, and he is coming."

—Revelation 4:8

After removing Saul, [God] made David their king. He testified concerning him: "I have found David son of Jesse, a man after my own heart; he will do everything I want him to do."

—Acts 13:22 NIV

Then David said to Nathan, "I have sinned against the Lord." Nathan answered, "The Lord has taken away your sin. You will not die."

—2 Samuel 12:13

Those who are in Christ Jesus are not judged guilty.

—Romans 8:1

A New Way of Thinking

Sometimes you have to think about homework. Sometimes you have to think about chores. But other times, you don't really *have* to think about anything in particular. Where does your mind go then? Do you daydream? Do you imagine things you'd like to do or friends you'd like to see? Do you worry?

You may not even be aware of all the things you think of, but *I* am. And I want to train you to think about Me. About who I am—Creator, Savior, King of kings. About My amazing, unending Love for you.

This new focus will take practice. Start by turning off the television and computer for a while and being quiet. Then ask My Spirit to help you. *Take My words to heart*, surrounding yourself with Scripture. Hang it on your wall, and sketch it on your notebooks. Talk to Me throughout your day. Simply pray, "Jesus, draw me close to You." As you do these things, you'll *be changed inside by a new way of thinking*.

I look at the heavens, which you made with your hands. I see the moon and stars, which you created. But why is man important to you? Why do you take care of human beings?

—Psalm 8:3–4

I have taken your words to heart so I would not sin against you.

—Psalm 119:11

Do not be shaped by this world. Instead be changed within by a new way of thinking. Then you will be able to decide what God wants for you. And you will be able to know what is good and pleasing to God and what is perfect.

—Romans 12:2

I AM YOUR RISEN, LIVING SAVIOR! Through My resurrection *you have been born again to an ever-living hope.*

—*JESUS LIVES*

Listen, I tell you this secret: We will not all die, but we will all be changed. It will only take a second. We will be changed as quickly as an eye blinks. This will happen when the last trumpet sounds. The trumpet will sound and those who have died will be raised to live forever. And we will all be changed.

—1 Corinthians 15:51–52

Love and Peace

I am *the God of Love and Peace*.

Let this wonderful truth sink into your heart, mind, and spirit. Come to Me when you need to feel My Love, and I'll wrap you up in it. Come to Me when you are worried or nervous or afraid. I will wipe all that away and fill you with My Peace. Curl up in *My arms*. Be safe and rest.

I want you to be more and more like Me. Give others the same love and peace I give you. If someone makes you angry, remember that I created everyone—even that person—*in My image*. Love anyway, and forgive quickly. I know it's not easy, but with My Spirit's help, you can do it! Forgiving will bring you peace. And don't forget to forgive yourself as well, because you'll make mistakes too. By living this way, you'll become more like Me, the God of Love and Peace.

Live in harmony. Do what I have asked you to do.
Agree with each other, and live in peace. Then
the God of love and peace will be with you.

—2 Corinthians 13:11

The everlasting God is your place of safety.
His arms will hold you up forever. He
will force your enemy out ahead of you.
He will say, "Destroy the enemy!"

—Deuteronomy 33:27

God created human beings in his image.
In the image of God he created them.
He created them male and female.

—Genesis 1:27

Come to Me with Courage

Be strong and brave. Put your hope in the Lord.

I want My children to be brave, not cowardly. In fact, the Bible warns against being a coward.

When you are going through really tough times and it seems like nothing will ever be right again, it's tempting to look for an easy way out. You may even start to feel sorry for yourself, thinking, *I don't deserve all this trouble.* But this kind of attitude *is* trouble! It means that you aren't trusting Me to take care of you.

Whatever you're dealing with may be hurtful and hard—a bully, trouble at home, or problems with a friend—but it's happening for a reason. Be brave! Trust that I am in control. Know that I am with you through all your struggles.

Come to Me with courage in your heart, putting your hope and faith in Me. When you do, I will bless you over and over, in so many different ways. I will make you stronger and braver than you've ever been.

All you who put your hope in the
Lord be strong and brave.
—Psalm 31:24

"Those who are cowards, who refuse to believe,
who do evil things, who kill, who are sexually
immoral, who do evil magic, who worship idols,
and who tell lies—all these will have a place in the
lake of burning sulfur. This is the second death."
—Revelation 21:8

Look, the Lord God is coming with power. He will
use his power to rule all the people. Look, he will
bring reward for his people. . . . The Lord takes care
of his people like a shepherd. He gathers the people
like lambs in his arms. He carries them close to
him. He gently leads the mothers of the lambs.
—Isaiah 40:10–11

What Your Heart Can See

We hope for something we have not yet seen, and we patiently wait for it. What is "it," this thing you have not yet seen? My promise of heaven.

You may be thinking, *How can we hope for something we cannot see?* That's an excellent question. Of our five senses, seeing is the one that people often value the most. I created a beautiful, glorious world, and I *do* want your eyes to enjoy all its wonders.

Yet there is another kind of seeing—with the eyes of your heart. Your heart has a spiritual eyesight that your eyes do not. It can "see" the hope of heaven—which is My promise to you.

As you travel through this world, train your eyes to notice My wonders within nature. But also train the eyes of your heart to notice the many unseen blessings of My Presence as you wait for heaven. Focus on Me—remembering that *faith means knowing something is real even if you don't see it.*

We hope for something we have not yet
seen, and we patiently wait for it.

—Romans 8:25 CEV

"I have given these people the glory that you
gave me. I gave them this glory so that they
can be one, the same as you and I are one."

—John 17:22

Faith means being sure of the things we
hope for. And faith means knowing that
something is real even if we do not see it.

—Hebrews 11:1

You Will Have Happiness

Don't be afraid to be happy. Because you are Mine, you *will* have some happiness—even in this mixed-up, messed-up world.

When you're happy, don't wonder how long it will last. Don't worry about what might happen next. Don't think about what you should be doing instead of having fun. Just enjoy this time—it is My gift to you.

You don't have to have every detail of your life perfectly planned out first. You can be happy even if you have a problem that still needs fixing. For this moment, though, just celebrate being with Me. *Be still*—relax—*and know that I am God.* The psalmist wrote: *Happy are the people whose God is the Lord.*

Simply smile and say, "Jesus, I am going to enjoy being with You—right here and right now!" After all, I enjoy being with you.

Happy are the people whose God is the Lord.
—Psalm 144:15

God says, "Be still, and know that I am God. I will be praised in all the nations. I will be praised throughout the earth."
—Psalm 46:10

God is our protection and our strength. He always helps in times of trouble. So we will not be afraid if the earth shakes, or if the mountains fall into the sea. We will not fear even if the oceans roar and foam, or if the mountains shake at the raging sea.
—Psalm 46:1–3

Made New

*Y*ou are being made new every day. That means every morning is another beginning. If you made a mistake yesterday—even if you really goofed everything up—it's okay. Yes, you may have some work to do to make things right with other people. But with Me, today is a fresh start.

Put yesterday's mistakes behind you, and focus on following Me today. As you do, I will *transform* you. I'll change you little by little so that you look just a bit more like Me each day.

You cannot make yourself new, no matter how hard you try or how good you are. That is something only My Spirit and I can do. Sometimes the changes will be simple; sometimes they'll be more difficult. Thank Me for them anyway. I will be with you every step, *holding your hand* the whole way.

We do not give up. Our physical body is becoming older and weaker, but our spirit inside us is made new every day.

—2 Corinthians 4:16

You are not ruled by your sinful selves. You are ruled by the Spirit, if that Spirit of God really lives in you. But if anyone does not have the Spirit of Christ, then he does not belong to Christ.

—Romans 8:9

But I am always with you. You have held my hand. You guide me with your advice. And later you will receive me in honor.

—Psalm 73:23–24

The Path

Because you are My child, the path of your life has a wonderful destination: heaven.

I am walking with you. I know every twist and turn on your path. You view problems as obstacles, potholes, and speed bumps that slow you down. But you only see a small part of the way. I see the whole thing. I know those bumps and problems will teach you lessons that will help you farther on down the path. Just take the next small step. Trust Me to lead you on an open road.

When you trust Me, you're walking by faith, and I am constantly with you. I'll never fail you or disappoint you! *I am the Way*, the only way to God. I died on the cross so that the path of Life—the path to Him—would be open for you. Keep walking, step after step—and thank Me for clearing the way to heaven for you.

The only temptations that you have are the temptations that all people have. But you can trust God. He will not let you be tempted more than you can stand. But when you are tempted, God will also give you a way to escape that temptation. Then you will be able to stand it.

—1 Corinthians 10:13

We live by what we believe, not by what we can see.

—2 Corinthians 5:7

Jesus answered, "I am the way. And I am the truth and the life. The only way to the Father is through Me."

—John 14:6

You will teach me God's way to live. Being with you will fill me with joy. At your right hand I will find pleasure forever.

—Psalm 16:11

Lord, help me to remember that nothing is going to happen to me today that You and I can't handle together. Amen.

O Sovereign LORD!
You made the
heavens and earth
by your strong
hand and powerful
arm. Nothing is
too hard for you!

—JEREMIAH 32:17 NLT

In the Middle of the Mess

You can find Joy in the middle of your toughest times. Sounds impossible, doesn't it? Especially when several problems come all at once. But nothing is impossible with Me!

Don't spend all your time trying to figure out how to fix your troubles. Instead, remember that I am with you. I am working in your life, as everything is going on. Because I am perfectly wise, I can bring good out of evil. I can outsmart the devil and anything this world throws at you.

The way to find Joy is to pray, "Jesus, help me see You in this mess!" It really is that simple. As you unplug from the problem and plug into My Presence, good things start to happen. Your dark mood grows lighter and brighter. And, as you *remain in Me*—connected to My Presence—you'll begin to see your struggles as I see them. And you'll have Joy in the middle of the mess.

You will have many kinds of troubles. But when these things happen, you should be very happy. You know that these things are testing your faith. And this will give you patience.

—James 1:2–3

Yes, God's riches are very great! God's wisdom and knowledge have no end! No one can explain the things God decides. No one can understand God's ways.

—Romans 11:33

"Remain in me, and I will remain in you. No branch can produce fruit alone. It must remain in the vine. It is the same with you. You cannot produce fruit alone. You must remain in me."

—John 15:4

The Sun

Trying to please Me is a wonderful, joyful way to live. Of course, *without faith, no one can please Me*. You must *believe that I am real and that I reward those who truly want to find Me*.

Living to please Me will bless you with rewards in heaven. You'll also be blessed with daily rewards on earth—like love, joy, peace, patience, and self-control.

I want to be the center of your world, just as the sun is the center of the solar system. But keeping Me at the center of your every thought, word, and action can be a challenge. It all begins with your thinking. You must *capture every thought and make it give up and obey Me*. Also, study My Word to find out what pleases Me. Make Me the Sun of your world—and let Me shine in your life.

Without faith no one can please God. Anyone who comes to God must believe that he is real and that he rewards those who truly want to find him.

—Hebrews 11:6

We destroy every proud thing that raises itself against the knowledge of God. We capture every thought and make it give up and obey Christ.

—2 Corinthians 10:5

We have continued praying for you. We ask God that you will know fully what God wants. We pray that you will also have great wisdom and understanding in spiritual things.

—Colossians 1:9

I Will Go Before You

I Myself will go before you. I will be with you. Don't be afraid. Don't worry. I am your loving Savior, and I am also your All-Powerful, Forever God! I am *omnipresent*—which means that I am everywhere, and in all times, all at once. This makes it possible for Me to go ahead of you in your day, smoothing out the way for you, without ever leaving your side.

No matter where you go or what troubles you go through, I *will* be with you. Because you know this, you can be brave and bold. Fear and worry may sometimes creep into your heart, but they don't belong there. Your heart is where *I* live. So check it from time to time. Are fear and worry hanging out there? If they are, ask the Holy Spirit to kick them out! Then cheer yourself up with this promise: *I will go before you. I will be with you*—and *My perfect Love takes away fear.*

The Lord himself will go before you. He will be with you. He will not leave you or forget you. Don't be afraid. Don't worry.

—Deuteronomy 31:8

I ask the Father in his great glory to give you the power to be strong in spirit. He will give you that strength through his Spirit. I pray that Christ will live in your hearts because of your faith. I pray that your life will be strong in love and be built on love.

—Ephesians 3:16–17

Where God's love is, there is no fear, because God's perfect love takes away fear. It is punishment that makes a person fear. So love is not made perfect in the person who has fear.

—1 John 4:18

Powerful Praise

Praise is powerful. It will not only get you through this day; it will give you victory over this day. When you worship Me with songs and words and prayers, we connect in the most powerful way. *Your praises are My throne*. Praising Me brings you into My Presence and gives you a glimpse of My Power and Glory.

The devil can't stand to hear your praises. So sing and shout them! They put him on the run. Worry, fear, and feeling sorry for yourself also vanish when you praise Me with all your heart. But the most important reason to worship Me is because I am *worthy to receive honor and glory and praise!*

No matter how dark and difficult your day may seem, your praises are powerful. They bring the Light of My Presence into your life and give you victory over your day!

You sit as the Holy One. The praises
of Israel are your throne.

—Psalm 22:3

"By his power we live and move and exist." Some of
your own poets have said: "For we are his children."

—Acts 17:28

Then I looked, and I heard the voices of many
angels. The angels were around the throne, the four
living things, and the elders. There were thousands
and thousands of angels—there were 10,000 times
10,000. The angels said in a loud voice: "The Lamb
who was killed is worthy to receive power, wealth,
wisdom and strength, honor, glory, and praise!"

—Revelation 5:11–12

No Surprises

Don't know what's going to happen tomorrow? That's okay, because I do. And I have everything you need to face it. Nothing—absolutely nothing—surprises Me. Not surprise parties, not pop quizzes, not accidents, not even the weather.

People want to be able to tell the future. Some of them even make a lot of money pretending that they *can* tell the future. But the future belongs to Me. And because it belongs to Me, you don't need to worry about it. Just keep your eyes on Me.

Too many people fear what the future may bring; they wonder if they'll be able to handle it. But that kind of thinking is a waste of time. Remember: I am working in your life right now. And *I will help you deal with whatever hard things come up when the time comes*. Because life has no surprises for Me.

"Give your entire attention to what God is doing right now, and don't get worked up about what may or may not happen tomorrow. God will help you deal with whatever hard things come up when the time comes."

—Matthew 6:34 the message

"The Spirit of the Lord is in me. This is because God chose me to tell the Good News to the poor. God sent me to tell the prisoners of sin that they are free, and to tell the blind that they can see again. God sent me to free those who have been treated unfairly."

—Luke 4:18

"The things I said would happen have happened. And now I tell you about new things. Before those things happen, I tell you about them."

—Isaiah 42:9

Lean on Me

Lean on Me as you go through your day.

Everyone leans on someone or something—even if they don't realize it. Some people lean on their friends or family. Others lean on themselves, thinking they are smart enough to handle whatever comes without any help. Still others lean on their beauty or their stuff or their popularity. These things aren't bad. In fact, they are all gifts from Me, and I want you to enjoy them. But depending on them is risky, because every one of them can let you down.

You don't have to pretend that you've got it all figured out, or that you're so strong you don't need help. You can rest all your weight on Me. I'm standing nearby, with My strong arm reaching out to you. I am offering you My help. Lean fully on Me—I will be *your Strength*, and I'll hold you up.

Some friends may ruin you. But a real
friend will be more loyal than a brother.

—Proverbs 18:24

I will sing about your strength. In the morning I
will sing about your love. You are my protection,
my place of safety in times of trouble. God, my
strength, I will sing praises to you. God, my
protection, you are the God who loves me.

—Psalm 59:16–17

It was by faith that Jacob blessed each
one of Joseph's sons. He did this while
he was dying. Then he worshiped as he
leaned on the top of his walking stick.

—Hebrews 11:21

What is trusting God?
It's being completely,
100 percent sure that
you can count on Him to
protect and take care of
you. It's knowing that He
will *never* let you down.
It's believing that He will
always do the very best for
you. And it's following Him
wherever He leads you.

So our hope is
in the Lord.
He is our help, our
shield to protect us.
We rejoice in him.
We trust his holy name.
Lord, show your
love to us
as we put our
hope in you.

—Psalm 33:20–22

My Protection

I watch over and *protect everyone who loves Me.* Let this promise of Mine comfort you. This promise is for *you* because you love Me.

You don't have to earn My protection. It is simply yours because you belong to Me. So when the thunder booms, when the bully threatens, or when anything at all frightens you, know that I am watching over you—*like a shepherd* watches over his flock.

Everyone likes to feel protected by someone who is bigger and stronger. I am bigger and stronger than any fear you'll ever face. Sometimes you may feel as if you're all alone and without anyone to look out for you—but you're not! Talk to Me, reach out to Me, and I will reach out to you with My watchful, loving Presence.

The Lord protects everyone who loves
him. But he will destroy the wicked.

—Psalm 145:20

We love because God first loved us.

—1 John 4:19

"Nations, listen to the message from the Lord.
Tell this message in the faraway lands by the
sea: 'The one who scattered the people of
Israel will bring them back together. And he
will watch over his people like a shepherd.'"

—Jeremiah 31:10

Trust God all the time. Tell him all your
problems. God is our protection.

—Psalm 62:8

Run to Me

I am the One who keeps you safe. I know you like to think and plan and figure things out on your own, searching for a way to feel secure. But beware of *trusting in yourself* and your own ideas. They aren't perfect. Only My plans for you are perfect. Trust Me.

When you're worried, your mind spins around and around and around, trying to figure out just the right answer to your problem. It can make you dizzy! Relax. I am with you the whole time, *holding your hand*.

I will always give you good advice. When you're confused about what to do, try writing out your prayers. Ask Me to show you what to do. Study My Word. Then wait quietly for Me to answer. I will be your *strong tower. Run to Me*, and I will keep you safe.

But I am always with you. You have held
my hand. You guide me with your advice.
And later you will receive me in honor.
—Psalm 73:23–24

The person who trusts in himself is foolish. But
the person who lives wisely will be kept safe.
—Proverbs 28:26

The Lord is like a strong tower. Those who
do what is right can run to him for safety.
—Proverbs 18:10

A Second Chance

A do-over, a second chance—that's what I'm offering you. I know you have messed up. *You* know you've messed up. But listen to this truth: *My love never ends. My mercies never stop. They are new every morning.*

What does that mean? It means you get to try again. Whatever mistakes you made yesterday are gone when you give them to Me and ask My forgiveness. Today is a new day and a fresh start. I know that can be hard to believe when you've made a really big mistake. But believe it. A second chance is My gift to you. And the greatest second chance of all is forever with Me in heaven.

Sometimes it can seem like your regrets and sadness will never end, but they will. Only My Love for you will never end. Trust it—and Me. Believe that I'll forgive you. Look to Me, accept My Love, and I will help you through this new day.

The Lord's love never ends. His mercies
never stop. They are new every morning.
Lord, your loyalty is great.

—Lamentations 3:22–23

The Lord makes me very happy. All that I am
rejoices in my God. The Lord has covered me with
clothes of salvation. He has covered me with a coat
of goodness. I am like a bridegroom dressed for
his wedding. I am like a bride dressed in jewels.

—Isaiah 61:10

"For God loved the world so much that he gave his
only Son. God gave his Son so that whoever believes
in him may not be lost, but have eternal life."

—John 3:16

Worry Is a Waste

What is worry? *Worry* is thinking about things at the wrong time. Your brain has the amazing ability to actually think about your own thoughts. I created you that way. And because you can think about what you're thinking about, you can also *choose* what you think about.

It's important not to waste your brainpower. If you give thought to certain things at the wrong times—like when you're trying to go to sleep—it's easy to start worrying about those things. Most likely, you can't do anything about them while you're lying in bed anyway. Worry just keeps you awake. What a waste!

So what should you do if you find yourself focused on certain things when you shouldn't be? Change your "worry" thoughts to "worship" thoughts. Don't think, *What should I do?* or *What will happen?* Think instead, *Thank You, Jesus! I know You'll take care of this! I know You'll take care of me!* Because I will.

Jesus said to his followers, "So I tell you, don't worry about the food you need to live. Don't worry about the clothes you need for your body. Life is more important than food. And the body is more important than clothes. Look at the birds. They don't plant or harvest. They don't save food in houses or barns. But God takes care of them. And you are worth much more than birds. None of you can add any time to your life by worrying about it. If you cannot do even the little things, then why worry about the big things?"

—Luke 12:22–26

Fear God and give him praise. The time has come for God to judge all people. Worship God. He made the heavens, the earth, the sea, and the springs of water.

—Revelation 14:7

Spend Time with Me

I will fill you with Joy and Peace when you trust Me. The best way to truly trust Me is to spend time with Me. Don't be too busy for Me. Friends are wonderful and games are great, but don't forget to save time for Me.

Just as having hours upon hours with friends makes you better friends, the more you are with Me, the closer we will be. You'll start to look forward to our time together—in the same way you look forward to being with your best friend.

Something else happens as we spend time together too—you become more like Me. Because you belong to Me, My Spirit lives in you. And He is always working to *change you to be like Me.* As you grow, hope grows inside you. Soon it fills you up and overflows—spilling out and splashing Peace and Joy into the lives of everyone around you.

I pray that the God who gives hope will fill you with much joy and peace while you trust in him. Then your hope will overflow by the power of the Holy Spirit.

—Romans 15:13

You, Lord, give true peace. You give peace to those who depend on you. You give peace to those who trust you.

—Isaiah 26:3

You are not ruled by your sinful selves. You are ruled by the Spirit, if that Spirit of God really lives in you.

—Romans 8:9

We all show the Lord's glory, and we are being changed to be like him. This change in us brings more and more glory. And it comes from the Lord, who is the Spirit.

—2 Corinthians 3:18

Sing to Me

Sing to Me, because I have taken care of you. Sometimes singing praises is the last thing you feel like doing. But that's probably when you need to sing most! I am *always* taking care of you—even though some days it may not seem that way.

There will be moments when you'll wish My plan for you wasn't so hard! But hard times aren't a mistake in My plan, and they don't mean My Love for you is gone. I'm working to bring you closer to Me and to make you stronger. Like an athlete in training, you need to learn to keep running when you're tired and to keep climbing when you feel like giving up. That's what tough times are teaching you to do.

You don't really know what your friends are facing, so don't compare your life with theirs. And don't give up when you're tired—follow Me! I will help you see all the ways I care for you and protect you. *Sing to Me!* Through your praises, I give you hope and make you strong.

I sing to the Lord because
he has taken care of me.

—Psalm 13:6

God is my protection. He makes my way
free from fault. He makes me like a
deer, which does not stumble. He helps
me stand on the steep mountains.

—2 Samuel 22:33–34

Jesus answered, "Perhaps I want him to
live until I come back. That should not be
important to you. You follow me!"

—John 21:22

To be a
Christian
without prayer
is no more
possible than
to be alive
without
breathing.

—Martin Luther

I keep the
Lord before
me always.
Because he
is close by
my side
I will not
be hurt.

—Psalm 16:8

Choose Joy Instead

Be full of joy in Me always. Let everyone see that you are gentle and kind.

There is no shortage of things to complain about—friends acting weird, too much homework, your terrible lunch. Instead of complaining, choose joy. Choose to remember My Goodness. That will help you keep the whining away.

I understand that getting grouchy seems like the thing to do when life isn't going your way. It's tempting to talk back to your mom or snap at a friend. But I want you to be gentle and kind—especially when you'd rather be grouchy.

Be happy. Why? Simply because *I am near*—invisible yet constantly with you. *I am the same yesterday, today, and forever*, so there is always something to praise Me for. Let Me smooth away your frustrations and grumpiness as you think about Me and all I do for you. Remember *My Love*, and choose joy instead!

Be full of joy in the Lord always. I
will say again, be full of joy.
Let all men see that you are gentle and
kind. The Lord is coming soon.

—Philippians 4:4–5

The Spirit gives love, joy, peace, patience, kindness,
goodness, faithfulness, gentleness, self-control.
There is no law that says these things are wrong.

—Galatians 5:22–23

Jesus Christ is the same yesterday,
today, and forever.

—Hebrews 13:8

Whoever is wise will remember these things.
He will think about the love of the Lord.

—Psalm 107:43

Changing You

You are being changed to be like Me. That is what My Spirit—who lives in you—does. He changes you, and it is an amazing work! But you have to allow those changes to happen.

How? By asking Me to use your hard times. Don't let them be wasted. I can use them to build up your courage, your patience, kindness, and self-control. In order to make you more like Me, you must be willing to *suffer as I suffered.* Then you *will have glory as I have glory.*

At times, you may think your troubles will never end. But even your biggest troubles are small compared to the Joy of heaven they're preparing you for. That's how I can ask you to praise Me on your worst days, and not just your best ones: because I know what I'm doing for you. I'm changing you to be more like Me. And I'm preparing you for a Joy that will last forever and ever!

Our faces, then, are not covered. We all show the Lord's glory, and we are being changed to be like him. This change in us brings more and more glory. And it comes from the Lord, who is the Spirit.

—2 Corinthians 3:18

If we are God's children, then we will receive the blessings God has for us. We will receive these things from God together with Christ. But we must suffer as Christ suffered, and then we will have glory as Christ has glory.

—Romans 8:17

We have small troubles for a while now, but they are helping us gain an eternal glory. That glory is much greater than the troubles.

—2 Corinthians 4:17

Always give thanks to God the Father for everything, in the name of our Lord Jesus Christ.

—Ephesians 5:20

Remember My Names

Remember Me while you are lying in bed. Think about Me through the night.

When you are trying to drift off to sleep, all kinds of thoughts can come flying at you from different directions. *How will I do on that test tomorrow? Is my friend mad at me? What is that shadow in the corner?* It's easy to start to worry. Grab hold of those thoughts and toss them to Me instead. *Give all your worries to Me, because I care for you.*

Remember who I am and let these truths encourage you: I am powerful, wise, and full of mercy. Find comfort in thinking about My Names: Shepherd, Savior, Prince of Peace. I am King above all kings and Lord over all lords. I am Love. I am always with you, and I watch over you while you sleep.

I am taking care of you! Just as a baby bird snuggles under the protection of its mother's wing, you can snuggle up in My Presence and sleep.

I remember you while I'm lying in bed.
I think about you through the night.

—Psalm 63:6

Give all your worries to him,
because he cares for you.

—1 Peter 5:7

You are my help. Because of your protection, I sing.

—Psalm 63:7

A child will be born to us. God will give a son to
us. He will be responsible for leading the people.
His name will be Wonderful Counselor, Powerful
God, Father Who Lives Forever, Prince of Peace.

—Isaiah 9:6

When You Wonder Why

There are days when things just don't make sense. And you wonder, *Why?*

When *Why?* is all you can think, trust Me. When you have no idea what to do, trust Me. I love this kind of trust, because I know it's real.

No one else may understand exactly what you're going through, but I do. I understand perfectly. You are not alone. *I am with you, and I will protect you everywhere you go.*

I never get tired. I never run out of energy or strength. So ask Me to work out your troubles for you. Things may get bumpy at times, but there is a way out—I will show it to you at just the right time. Instead of trying to fix things on your own, say this prayer: "I trust You, Jesus. Help me, Holy Spirit." When the bumpy times come, cling even tighter to Me. I won't let you fall. I will hold you up *with My right hand.*

"I am with you, and I will protect you everywhere you go. And I will bring you back to this land. I will not leave you until I have done what I have promised you."
—Genesis 28:15

"I will send you the Helper from the Father. He is the Spirit of truth who comes from the Father. When he comes, he will tell about me."
—John 15:26

I stay close to you. You support me with your right hand.
—Psalm 63:8

I Give You Power

I give you Power and Strength. I give you everything you need to face *anything*—good or bad. But to get My Power, you must stay close to Me.

You may not feel strong right this minute, but when trouble comes—and when you trust Me to take care of it—there is no need to be afraid. I'll make sure you are ready for what happens.

I carefully control everything that takes place in your life. I am constantly protecting you from both known and unknown dangers. I will not let anything touch you that you and I can't handle together through My Power. So trust Me. Keep telling yourself this truth: *"I can do all things through Christ because he gives me strength!"* I will give you Power!

I can do all things through Christ
because he gives me strength.

—Philippians 4:13

"Remain in me, and I will remain in you. No
branch can produce fruit alone. It must remain
in the vine. It is the same with you. You cannot
produce fruit alone. You must remain in me."

—John 15:4

The Lord is my strength and shield. I trust
him, and he helps me. I am very happy.
And I praise him with my song.

—Psalm 28:7

Waiting in Hope

*W*e wait in hope for the Lord; he is our help and our shield. But just waiting is not necessarily a good thing. *How* you wait is very important.

There is good waiting, and there is bad waiting. The bad kind is huffing and puffing, stomping your foot impatiently, and growing angry. Good waiting is more like watching—watching to see what I will do. I will do just the right thing at just the right time. That kind of waiting is called *hope*.

While you are watching and waiting and hoping, remember *I am your Help and your Shield*. I protect you. I am always ready to help you. Just ask Me! I have already shielded you from many hard things—things you never knew about because I didn't let them near you. So keep hoping and trusting. The Light of My Presence will shine in your life while you wait.

We wait in hope for the Lᴏʀᴅ; he
is our help and our shield.
—Psᴀʟᴍ 33:20 ɴɪᴠ

Then Jesus came to them and said, "All power
in heaven and on earth is given to me. So go
and make followers of all people in the world.
Baptize them in the name of the Father and
the Son and the Holy Spirit. Teach them to
obey everything that I have told you. You can
be sure that I will be with you always. I will
continue with you until the end of the world."
—Mᴀᴛᴛʜᴇᴡ 28:18–20

But I am like an olive tree growing in God's
Temple. I trust God's love forever and ever.
—Psᴀʟᴍ 52:8

I am your Lord! I am the Friend who is always with you, but you must remember that I am also your Lord. I am King over all. And I want to be the King of your life.

—*Jesus Calling: 365 Devotions for Kids*

The Lord is
all I have,
and so in him
I put my hope.

—Lamentations 3:24 GNT

Know That You Need Me

People who know they have great spiritual needs are happy. The kingdom of heaven belongs to them. That can be a difficult promise to understand. But what it means is that when you know you need Me, you should be happy. Why? Because so many people in this world live their whole lives never understanding that I am what they need. They miss out on My love, My help, My mercy, and My grace. They miss out on the power of My Spirit working in their lives. They miss out on heaven, because they don't depend on Me. So if you know you need Me, be happy!

You have been saved by grace because you believe— because you have faith. Both grace and faith are gifts from Me! You only have to accept them and thank Me for them.

Because you believe, heaven is yours. If this world gets you down, don't feel sorry for yourself. Instead say, "I am happy, because Jesus is mine and I am His!"

"Those people who know they have great
spiritual needs are happy. The kingdom
of heaven belongs to them."

—Matthew 5:3

I mean that you have been saved by grace
because you believe. You did not save
yourselves. It was a gift from God.

—Ephesians 2:8

Thanks be to God for his gift that
is too wonderful to explain.

—2 Corinthians 9:15

You guide me with your advice. And
later you will receive me in honor.

—Psalm 73:24

The Light of the World

I am the Light of the world. My followers will never live in darkness. They will have the Light that gives life.

There is a lot of darkness in this world. Not the kind that falls at night, but the kind that comes because there is sin and evil in the world. You've seen it on the news. You've seen it in your neighborhood. You've probably even felt it in your own life—bullies, hurt feelings, troubles at school or at home. Still, you can have Light in your life.

My Light goes before you like the world's most powerful flashlight, showing the path I want you to follow. And one day—because you love Me—that path will lead you all the way to heaven. There, My Light will shine in *all* its glory. *There will never be night again.* Live close to Me, and *I will give you light* for your life.

Later, Jesus talked to the people again. He said, "I am the light of the world. The person who follows me will never live in darkness. He will have the light that gives life."

—John 8:12

The way of the good person is like the light of dawn. It grows brighter and brighter until it is full daylight.

—Proverbs 4:18

There will never be night again. They will not need the light of a lamp or the light of the sun. The Lord God will give them light. And they will rule like kings forever and ever.

—Revelation 22:5

I Will Help You

I am your Help in times of trouble. My Presence is always with you, but I am *very* present in *times of trouble.*

You are a part of My royal family, and I promise to take care of you. When you're stressed, your heart may pound and your blood may race. What's happening in your body can keep you from feeling My Presence. Be still for just a second and simply say, "Jesus is here with me. I *know* He is here. He will help me through this." Then take a slow, deep breath—and another and another. Feel Me with you, making you stronger.

When David faced Goliath, I protected him. When Daniel was thrown to the lions, I shut their mouths. When Esther needed to be brave, I gave her courage. And when you need Me, I *will* help you.

I am still working in this world. You won't hear about it on the news or read it in the newspaper. But I'm still helping My people, and I *will* help you!

God is our protection and our strength.
He always helps in times of trouble.

—PSALM 46:1

The Lord your God caused the water to stop
flowing. The river was dry until the people
finished crossing it. The Lord did the same thing
for us at the Jordan that he did for the people
at the Red Sea. Remember that he stopped
the water at the Red Sea so we could cross.

—JOSHUA 4:23

God is strong and can help you not to fall. He can
bring you before his glory without any wrong in
you and give you great joy. He is the only God. He is
the One who saves us. To him be glory, greatness,
power, and authority through Jesus Christ our
Lord for all time past, now, and forever. Amen.

—JUDE vv. 24–25

Worship Me

*W*orship Me because I am holy. My holiness is beautiful.

There are many beautiful things in this world—flowers, sunsets, people—but none of them are perfectly holy. Only *I* am perfectly holy, without even a speck of sin. The beauty of My holiness is something you cannot completely understand right now—you can only see part of it. Someday, in heaven, you will *clearly* see all of it. For now though, you can think about My holiness and let it amaze you.

The angels sing, *"Holy, holy, holy is the Lord of heaven's armies. His glory fills the whole earth."* Join with them and worship Me! Worshiping Me changes you. You grow more and more into the person I created you to be.

Worship Me because of who I am. Read My Word so that you can know Me better and praise Me well. By understanding more of who I am, you are changed and I am glorified. And that is beautiful worship.

Praise the Lord for the glory of his name.
Worship the Lord because he is holy.

—Psalm 29:2

Now we see as if we are looking into a dark
mirror. But at that time, in the future, we shall
see clearly. Now I know only a part. But at that
time I will know fully, as God has known me.

—1 Corinthians 13:12

Each creature was calling to the others:
"Holy, holy, holy is the Lord of heaven's
armies. His glory fills the whole earth."

—Isaiah 6:3

You Belong to Me!

I *have called you by name, and you are Mine.* No matter how alone you may feel sometimes, you belong to Me! I bought you with My blood. I have already paid for your sins.

Nothing can separate you from My Love. Not one thing. And while I have millions and millions of followers, you are not just another person to Me. I know *you*. I know your name, and I always speak to you by name. In fact, you are so precious to Me that *I have written your name on My hand.*

You will have good days and not-so-good days. But no matter what kind of day it is, tell yourself this truth: "Jesus is with me, and He is in control." Believing this will make all the difference—not just for today, but for always.

Now this is what the Lord says. He created you, people of Jacob. He formed you, people of Israel. He says, "Don't be afraid, because I have saved you. I have called you by name, and you are mine."

—ISAIAH 43:1

Yes, I am sure that nothing can separate us from the love God has for us. Not death, not life, not angels, not ruling spirits, nothing now, nothing in the future, no powers, nothing above us, nothing below us, or anything else in the whole world will ever be able to separate us from the love of God that is in Christ Jesus our Lord.

—ROMANS 8:38–39

"See, I have written your name on my hand. Jerusalem, I always think about your walls."

—ISAIAH 49:16

I Will Give You Strength

I—*the Lord God*—*give you your strength.* You know you can't handle everything on your own, as much as you might want to. The good news is that you don't have to. Knowing that you need Me is actually a very good thing, a blessing. It keeps you turning to Me and letting Me use My *wonderful riches* to *give you everything you need*.

When you're tired and weak, turn to Me—the source of *your Strength*. Sometimes I will instantly pour My Power into you. Other times, I will make you stronger bit by bit, giving you just enough strength to do the next right thing. This is My way of keeping you close to Me, talking to Me, and leaning on Me.

When you are close to Me, you can hear Me whisper how much I love you. Trust Me—the Lord God—and I will give you strength.

The Lord God gives me my strength. He makes me like a deer, which does not stumble. He leads me safely on the steep mountains.

—Habakkuk 3:19

My God will use his wonderful riches in Christ Jesus to give you everything you need.

—Philippians 4:19

The Lord has glory and majesty. He has power and beauty in his Temple. Praise the Lord, all nations on earth. Praise the Lord's glory and power.

—Psalm 96:6–7

Nothing can
separate you
from God's love,
absolutely nothing.
God is enough
for time, God is
enough for eternity.
God is enough!

—HANNAH WHITALL SMITH

You have given
me many troubles
and bad times.
But you will give
me life again. . . .
You will make me
greater than ever.
And you will
comfort me again.

—Psalm 71:20–21

Always Be Happy

I want you to lean on Me—to need Me—happily and with joy.

Some people can't stand to need anyone else. They want to do everything all by themselves. But that is not My way! I designed you to need Me *all the time*. And I created you to find happiness and Joy when you turn to Me.

The apostle Paul said to *always be happy* and *to never stop praying*. You can talk to Me anytime, about anything. I don't need fancy words or long prayers. I promise that I will always hear you and that I will always care.

You can also show that you depend on Me by studying My Word to learn more about who I am and who I want you to be. Ask Me to use what you read to change you.

When you're with Me—talking to Me, listening to Me, just being still and knowing that I am God—you will find Joy. *Seek your happiness in Me.*

Always be happy. Never stop praying.
—1 Thessalonians 5:16–17

The Lord himself will go before you. He
will be with you. He will not leave you or
forget you. Don't be afraid. Don't worry.
—Deuteronomy 31:8

With all my heart I try to obey you, God. Don't let
me break your commands. I have taken your words
to heart so I would not sin against you. Lord, you
should be praised. Teach me your demands.
—Psalm 119:10–12

Seek your happiness in the Lord, and he
will give you your heart's desire.
—Psalm 37:4 GNT

Live in My Light

Live in the Light of My Presence. Rejoice in My Name all the time. Praise My Goodness.

This world is getting darker and darker, but the Light of My Presence is as bright as ever. In fact, the Light of My Glory shines even more brightly against the darkness of evil. When My Goodness crashes into worldly evil, look out! There will be miracles! I will show My Power and Might and Goodness in this world.

Rejoice in My Name—no matter what is happening. Use My Name—*Jesus*—as a whispered prayer, as a praise, as a protection. It never loses its power. And by that power, I give you My Righteousness, covering you with My Salvation like a robe.

This is how you live in My Light: by calling on My Name and by wearing the robe of My Salvation with joy!

Happy are the people who know how to praise you. Lord, let them live in the light of your presence. In your name they rejoice all the time. They praise your goodness.

—Psalm 89:15–16

So God raised Christ to the highest place. God made the name of Christ greater than every other name. God wants every knee to bow to Jesus—everyone in heaven, on earth, and under the earth. Everyone will say, "Jesus Christ is Lord" and bring glory to God the Father.

—Philippians 2:9–11

The Lord makes me very happy. All that I am rejoices in my God. The Lord has covered me with clothes of salvation. He has covered me with a coat of goodness.

—Isaiah 61:10

Your Shield and Your Shepherd

I am a *Shield to those who trust Me*. Just as an umbrella shields you from the rain, I will shield you from danger and fear. So come close to Me. Stay under the covering of My Presence.

Whenever you forget that I am with you, you try to face the world on your own—without Me—and you leave My umbrella of protection. At the moment you feel that first tingle of fear that you are all alone, take it as your warning! Come back to Me. Say, "I trust You, Jesus."

Shielding you from danger and fear is part of My job because *I am your Shepherd*. I'm always watching over you. I know everything that will happen *before* it happens. So I'll make sure you have everything you need—strength, courage, and protection. I am taking care of you!

A good shepherd guides his sheep so carefully that they never know all the dangers he has saved them from. I am the only *Good Shepherd* for you. Follow Me. Let Me be your Shield.

The ways of God are without fault. The Lord's words are pure. He is a shield to those who trust him.
—2 Samuel 22:31

The Lord is my shepherd. I have everything I need. He gives me rest in green pastures. He leads me to calm water. He gives me new strength. For the good of his name, he leads me on paths that are right. Even if I walk through a very dark valley, I will not be afraid because you are with me. Your rod and your shepherd's staff comfort me.
—Psalm 23:1–4

"I am the good shepherd. The good shepherd gives his life for the sheep. . . . I am the good shepherd. I know my sheep, and my sheep know me, just as the Father knows me, and I know the Father. I give my life for the sheep."
—John 10:11, 14–15

Live the Life

I *want you to live the life I have given you to live*—and to be content with it. Being *content* means finding happiness in the life and things you have. Don't compare your life, or the things you have, to anyone else's. And don't look back and regret that your situation is different from what it used to be.

This life I have given you may not always be easy. But I'll make sure you have everything you need to live it fully. I'll even help you find Joy and Happiness in it! Being content won't just happen. You have to choose it. You have to look for Me.

This doesn't mean you can't hope for a better future. Contentment simply means trusting My plan for you—even if you don't always understand it.

As you learn to trust Me more and more, you'll not only find that you are happy with your life—you'll also find that your life is full of Joy.

Each one of you should continue to live the way God has given him to live—the way he was when God called him. This is a rule I make in all the churches.

—1 Corinthians 7:17

I know how to live when I am poor. And I know how to live when I have plenty. I have learned the secret of being happy at any time in everything that happens. . . . I have learned to be happy when I have all that I need and when I do not have the things I need.

—Philippians 4:12

Yes, God's riches are very great! God's wisdom and knowledge have no end! No one can explain the things God decides. No one can understand God's ways. As the Scripture says, "Who has known the mind of the Lord? Who has been able to give the Lord advice?" "No one has ever given God anything that he must pay back." Yes, God made all things. And everything continues through God and for God.

—Romans 11:33–36

I Never Vanish

I give strength to My people. I bless My people with Peace. "My people" are all those who trust Me as their Savior and God.

When you're feeling tired and weak, don't waste your energy worrying about whether or not you can handle all the stuff you're facing. I am All-Knowing, so I already know everything you will go through. And I'm ready to help you—every step of the way. I will give you My Strength.

Because you are Mine, I will also give you My Peace. The world's peace lasts only as long as everything is going your way. As soon as something goes wrong, it vanishes! My Peace is different. It doesn't depend on what happens—it depends on Me, and I never vanish! My Peace stays with you, in good times and bad—because I stay with you, in good times and bad.

The Lord gives strength to his people. The
Lord blesses his people with peace.

—Psalm 29:11

"For God loved the world so much that he gave his
only Son. God gave his Son so that whoever believes
in him may not be lost, but have eternal life."

—John 3:16

"I leave you peace. My peace I give you. I do not
give it to you as the world does. So don't let
your hearts be troubled. Don't be afraid."

—John 14:27

And God's peace will keep your hearts and
minds in Christ Jesus. The peace that God gives
is so great that we cannot understand it.

—Philippians 4:7

A Great Adventure

You are on a great adventure with Me. Like any adventure, it won't always go smoothly, but it will be good! There will be blessings as well as struggles. There is so much I want to teach you as we journey together. Be willing to try new—and sometimes hard—things. Say "Yes!" to stepping out in faith with Me.

I will give you everything you need for the journey. Don't waste time and energy trying to figure out what might come up in the future. I have the power to give you anything. I even have an army of angels ready to do whatever I command.

Never stop praying as you make decisions about this journey. Because I already know what your future will be, I'll help you make good choices today.

You may think up lots of different plans for your life, but remember who is really in charge. *I am the Lord. I decide what you will do.*

There are some things the Lord our God
has kept secret. But there are some things
he has let us know. . . . It is so we will
do everything in these teachings.

—Deuteronomy 29:29

He has put his angels in charge of you.
They will watch over you wherever you go.
They will catch you with their hands. And
you will not hit your foot on a rock.

—Psalm 91:11–12

Never stop praying.

—1 Thessalonians 5:17

A person may think up plans. But the
Lord decides what he will do.

—Proverbs 16:9

I will live
for God. . . .
If no one
else does,
I still will.

—Jonathan Edwards

"I am
the Lord.
I do not
change."

—MALACHI 3:6

Hold on to Me

I care for you. I am always thinking about you and watching over you. I am God, and I never forget about you.

You are only human, and sometimes you forget Me—especially when you're weak or tired or scared. I understand. When you find that your heart and mind have wandered away from Me, forgive yourself. Then hurry back! Say My Name, praise Me, or sing to Me—and you'll be right back with Me again. Then, *give all your worries to Me*. Worries and fears are like buzzing flies. They roam in and out of your mind whenever they want to. Capture them and give them to Me.

Trust Me to help you. I know everything that's happening in your life. I can help you because *all power in heaven and on earth is given to Me*. Let go of your worries and cares—and hold on to Me.

Give all your worries to him,
because he cares for you.
—1 Peter 5:7

Then Jesus came to them and said, "All power
in heaven and on earth is given to me."
—Matthew 28:18

At that time the followers came to Jesus and asked,
"Who is greatest in the kingdom of heaven?"
Jesus called a little child to him. He stood the
child before the followers. Then he said, "I tell
you the truth. You must change and become
like little children. If you don't do this, you
will never enter the kingdom of heaven."
—Matthew 18:1–3

Fuel for You

My Love will never fail you. It is your "fuel"—the best source of energy for you. It will never run out. My Love will help you keep going, keep doing the right things. Because there *will* be times when you get tired of doing what is right. Maybe it's because you think no one notices the good you do. Or maybe it's because everyone else seems to be doing wrong. Or perhaps doing the right thing doesn't seem to make a difference.

In any of these situations, take some time to focus on Me rather than getting frustrated. Let Me "fuel" you up. Because the more you think about and trust Me, the more you will be filled with My Love, My Strength, and My Power. They'll pour into you, so that you can pour them out on others—and keep doing good things.

We must not become tired of doing good.
We will receive our harvest of eternal life
at the right time. We must not give up!

—GALATIANS 6:9

He loves what is right and fair. The
Lord's love fills the earth.

—PSALM 33:5

Be full of joy in the Lord always.

—PHILIPPIANS 4:4

To do this, I work and struggle, using Christ's
great strength that works so powerfully in me.

—COLOSSIANS 1:29

If someone says, "I believe that Jesus is the
Son of God," then God lives in him. And he
lives in God. And so we know the love that
God has for us, and we trust that love.

—1 JOHN 4:15–16

Good Plans

Some people are afraid of the future. But I promise you that yours will be great. *I have good plans for you. I plan to give you hope and a future.*

Your future is better than anything you could ever imagine! Because when you choose to follow Me, your future is heaven.

Heaven is the most amazingly perfect place. Knowing that you are on your way there is very important. It will help you every day, every second of your life. Because even though living in heaven is in your future, the Light of heaven shines in your life today.

When I died on the cross, I took the punishment for all your sin. I also became your unfailing Hope—your never-ending Promise—of heaven. No matter what is happening in your life, keep looking to Me in hope. As you trust Me, the Light of heaven will shine in your heart and light up your life.

"I say this because I know what I have planned for you," says the Lord. "I have good plans for you. I don't plan to hurt you. I plan to give you hope and a good future."

—JEREMIAH 29:11

Why am I so sad? Why am I so upset? I should put my hope in God. I should keep praising him, My Savior and my God.

—PSALM 42:5–6

God once said, "Let the light shine out of the darkness!" And this is the same God who made his light shine in our hearts. He gave us light by letting us know the glory of God that is in the face of Christ.

—2 CORINTHIANS 4:6

Ugly Thoughts and Things

The world is filled with ugly things. Big problems, little problems, what you hear at school, what you see on the news. All these ugly things seem to shout, "Think about me!" They can make you so *tired* that you *stop trying* to follow Me.

But you can *choose* what you think about. Ask Me to sweep out all the ugly thoughts and fill your mind with My Light and Love—and I will.

Sometimes those ugly thoughts are about mistakes you made months or years ago. Don't let the past mess up today. This very moment is a chance to start over. Tell Me you're sorry, and I *will* forgive you.

Ugly thoughts are sneaky. They creep in when you aren't paying attention. Some days, you may have to pray hundreds of times: "Jesus, I want to see *You* in the middle of my problems." That's okay! Don't give up! *In this world you will have trouble. But be brave! I have defeated the world!*

Think about Jesus. He held on patiently while sinful men were doing evil things against him. Look at Jesus' example so that you will not get tired and stop trying.

—Hebrews 12:3

This poor man called, and the Lord heard him. The Lord saved him from all his troubles. The Lord saves those who fear him. His angel camps around them.

—Psalm 34:6–7

"I told you these things so that you can have peace in me. In this world you will have trouble. But be brave! I have defeated the world!"

—John 16:33

Your God and Your Guide

Take time to *think about My Love for you.* It never fails. *I am your God forever and ever. I will guide you from now on.*

Ask the Holy Spirit to help you think about My Presence with you whenever your mind starts to wander. Remember the words of Jacob from the Bible: *"Surely the Lord is in this place."* Know that I am here in *this* place with you too. Be happy that I am your God—today, tomorrow, and forever.

I am also your Guide. It's easy to be spooked by the future, especially when you forget that I am with you. But when you trust Me to be your Savior, I'll lead you through every step of your life. You can always draw closer to Me in the moment by simply whispering My Name. Later, when you have more time, tell Me everything that's happening. Yes, I already know, but I love listening to you. I am your God and your Guide—now and always.

God, we come into your Temple. There we think about your love. God, your name is known everywhere. Everywhere on earth people praise you. Your right hand is full of goodness. . . . This God is our God forever and ever. He will guide us from now on.

—Psalm 48:9–10, 14

Then Jacob woke from his sleep. He said, "Surely the Lord is in this place. But I did not know it."

—Genesis 28:16

Do not worry about anything. But pray and ask God for everything you need. And when you pray, always give thanks.

—Philippians 4:6

102

I Will Give You Victory

I am taking care of you. I know how hard this is to believe when you're having a bad day—especially when your bad day just seems to keep getting worse and worse! You might even start to feel as if I'm letting you down. You might wonder if I really care about your troubles. *God could fix everything with one word*, you think. *Why doesn't He?*

Though you may not understand how, I *am* loving you and I *am* working in your life. Sometimes My *ways* are a mystery, but My Love for you is not. It is always perfect and always yours. Rest in this wonderful Love.

Rather than trying to control things or think through your problems, close your eyes. Curl up in My Presence. Take a deep breath and let My Love surround you. Trust Me. I am *God your Savior*. And *I will give you victory*.

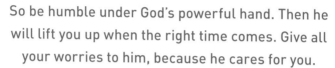

So be humble under God's powerful hand. Then he will lift you up when the right time comes. Give all your worries to him, because he cares for you.

—1 Peter 5:6–7

God says, "Be still and know that I am God. I will be praised in all the nations. I will be praised throughout the earth."

—Psalm 46:10

The Lord answered, "I myself will go with you. And I will give you victory."

—Exodus 33:14

I will look to the Lord for help. I will wait for God to save me. My God will hear me.

—Micah 7:7

Do not look to your hope, but to Christ, the source of your hope.

—Charles Spurgeon

"But the person who trusts in the Lord will be blessed. The Lord will show him that he can be trusted. He will be strong, like a tree planted near water. That tree has large roots that find the water. It is not afraid when the days are hot. Its leaves are always green. It does not worry in a year when no rain comes. That tree always produces fruit."

JEREMIAH 17:7–8

More Like Me

Y̶ou can *have joy with your troubles because you know that these troubles produce patience. And patience produces character, and character produces hope.*

It seems almost silly to say that you can have joy with your troubles. That's not the way the world thinks at all! But My way is very different from the world's way. When something is hurting you, look to My Spirit as He shows you what to do.

As you and I work through your troubles together, you'll learn patience. Patience is a rare thing these days. With microwaves, instant downloads, and fast food, people want everything to be easy and *right now!* But My ways take time. Learning patience will make your character more like Mine.

The more you become like Me, the more you'll have hope making you stronger each day. And you'll *know* that you belong to me. You'll also know that no matter what happens, there is nothing you and I can't handle together!

And we also have joy with our troubles because
we know that these troubles produce patience.
And patience produces character, and character
produces hope. And this hope will never disappoint
us, because God has poured out his love to fill
our hearts. God gave us his love through the
Holy Spirit, whom God has given to us.

—Romans 5:3–5

"If you love me, you will do the things I command. I will
ask the Father, and he will give you another Helper.
He will give you this Helper to be with you forever. The
Helper is the Spirit of truth. The world cannot accept
him because it does not see him or know him. But you
know him. He lives with you and he will be in you."

—John 14:15–17

I can do all things through Christ
because he gives me strength.

—Philippians 4:13

Putting Down the Pebbles

Imagine that you're standing at the edge of the ocean on a beach covered with pebbles. Each pebble represents a problem—yours, your family's, your friend's, the world's. You reach down and pick up one tiny stone. You hold it close to your eyes, looking at all the details. It's so close that you can no longer see the beauty of the ocean. At last, you put that pebble down, but then you pick up another.

In the same way, by looking only at your problems, you miss the beauty of My Presence. Put down your troubles long enough to receive My help.

I am like the ocean—endless and amazing. I'm asking you to put down all the pebbles of problems. Then you'll be able to "see" Me and feel My Love. Draw closer to Me by praying, "I choose *You*, Jesus. I choose to see You—not the problems." Keep doing this until it becomes a habit—a habit that keeps you close to Me.

So all of you, holy brothers, should think about Jesus. You were all called by God. God sent Jesus to us, and he is the high priest of our faith.

—Hebrews 3:1

He loves what is right and fair. The Lord's love fills the earth.

—Psalm 33:5

It was by faith that Moses left Egypt. He was not afraid of the king's anger. Moses continued strong as if he could see the God that no one can see.

—Hebrews 11:27

You will teach me God's way to live. Being with you will fill me with joy. At your right hand I will find pleasure forever.

—Psalm 16:11

I Am Big Enough!

I am *Immanuel—God with you*. And I am big enough to take care of you!

When life is good—friends are friendly, school is easy, and there aren't any troubles in sight—it's easy to trust Me. But when friends turn against you, school gets crazy, and there's a new trouble every time you turn around, you may wonder if I'm really able to take care of you after all. You may start to think of all the different ways *you* could make things better.

There's nothing wrong with trying to figure out how to solve a problem. Just don't forget to talk to Me about it. When your mind starts spinning, cranking out one possible answer after another, you can end up confused and exhausted. I can protect you from that. I can show you the next step to take.

Remember: *I will be with you always.* Choose to trust Me—every minute of each day. I am your Savior, and I am big enough to take care of you!

"She will give birth to a son. You will name the son Jesus. Give him that name because he will save his people from their sins." All this happened to make clear the full meaning of what the Lord had said through the prophet: "The virgin will be pregnant. She will have a son, and they will name him Immanuel." This name means "God is with us."

—Matthew 1:21–23

"Go and make followers. . . . Teach them to obey everything that I have told you. You can be sure that I will be with you always. I will continue with you until the end of the world."

—Matthew 28:19–20

There may be no olives growing on the trees. There may be no food growing in the fields. There may be no sheep in the pens. There may be no cattle in the barns. But I will still be glad in the Lord. I will rejoice in God my Savior.

—Habakkuk 3:17–18

Keep Holding On

Because you are Mine, the hope—the promise—of heaven belongs to you. *Hold on to this hope that I've given you.* Let it make you strong.

Imagine that you're playing outside on the swings, swinging high into the air. What happens if you don't grab on to the swing? You fall. But if you hold on tight, you soar! *You* have to do your part. *You* have to do the holding on. In the same way, *you* must cling to Me and My Hope. I'll take you higher and higher—but you have to hold on to Me.

To help you hold on, think about what I've *already* done for you (died for your sins), what I *am* doing (living in you), and what I *will* do (give you heaven). Let these thoughts encourage you. Keep trying! Hold tight to My Hope—and I will bless you!

These two things cannot change. God cannot lie
when he makes a promise, and he cannot lie when
he makes an oath. These things encourage us
who came to God for safety. They give us strength
to hold on to the hope we have been given.

—HEBREWS 6:18

I keep trying to reach the goal and get the prize.
That prize is mine because God called me through
Christ to the life above. All of us who have grown
spiritually to be mature should think this way,
too. And if there are things you do not agree with,
God will make them clear to you. But we should
continue following the truth we already have.

—PHILIPPIANS 3:14–16

I do not live anymore—it is Christ living in me. I
still live in my body, but I live by faith in the Son of
God. He loved me and gave himself to save me.

—GALATIANS 2:20

The Climb

Have you ever climbed a mountain, a steep hill, or a rocky slope? It can be hard to know where to put your foot. You don't want to slip and fall, so it's important to choose the right path.

Life can be like climbing a mountain. There are lots of different paths. Which is the right one? A path looks safe, but is it?

The mountain of life can sometimes seem impossible to climb. But *I am always with you. I am holding your hand. I will guide you. I will lead you safely on the steep mountains.*

The climb is sometimes easy and sometimes hard. But all along the way I've prepared gifts for you—like flowers in the cracks of the rocks. These gifts might be special friends, happy days with people you love, or a chance to help someone else. They remind you that I'm with you. Enjoy My gifts and enjoy traveling with Me. The climb isn't always easy, but the view is heavenly.

The Lord God gives me my strength. He makes
me like a deer, which does not stumble. He
leads me safely on the steep mountains.

—Habakkuk 3:19

But I am always with you. You have held
my hand. You guide me with your advice.
And later you will receive me in honor.

—Psalm 73:23–24

I saw the Lord. He was sitting on a very high throne.
His long robe filled the Temple. Burning heavenly
creatures stood above him. Each creature had six
wings. They used two wings to cover their faces.
They used two wings to cover their feet. And they
used two wings for flying. Each creature was
calling to the others: "Holy, holy, holy is the Lord of
heaven's armies. His glory fills the whole earth."

—Isaiah 6:1–3

On Holy Ground

Your mind is like a restless little puppy. It skips and scampers all over the place. Rarely does it stop. But all those thoughts skipping through your mind can make you tired.

Be still and listen for a moment. Hear Me saying, *"Come to Me."* I will give your mind rest. Just whisper My Name, and I'll help you grow quiet in My Presence. When you're with Me, you're on *holy ground*. I'll renew both your mind and your soul.

I'll also give you Hope—true Hope. The world only offers false hope and false promises. Many voices—on the TV, in advertisements, on the Internet—say, "This is the way!" Those voices want you to think about anything and everything except Me and My way. They make your mind skip and scamper. Don't listen to them! Come to Me. I'll give you rest—and the true Hope that comes from Me.

"Come to me, all of you who are tired and have heavy loads. I will give you rest. Accept my work and learn from me. I am gentle and humble in spirit. And you will find rest for your souls."

—Matthew 11:28–29

So Moses said, ". . . How can a bush continue burning without burning up?" The Lord saw Moses was coming to look at the bush. So God called to him from the bush, "Moses, Moses!" And Moses said, "Here I am." Then God said, "Do not come any closer. Take off your sandals. You are standing on holy ground."

—Exodus 3:3–5

I wait patiently for God to save me.
Only he gives me hope.

—Psalm 62:5

Everything
that is
done in
the world
is done
by hope.

—Martin Luther

I pray that the
God of peace
will give you
every good thing
you need so that
you can do
what he wants.

—Hebrews 13:20

Joy for All Times

I have done great things for you. Take time to think about all those marvelous things—and be amazed! I am the God who spun the stars out into the sky, who split the seas, and who died to save you.

I want to fill you up with My Joy—but you have to let Me. Don't be like that child on Christmas morning who rips open all the presents and then says, "Is that all?" Every single day is a precious gift from Me—filled with gifts for you! *Search for Me* and *you will find Me.*

My Joy and blessings aren't just for happy times; they are also for the tough times. When things are going your way, My Joy makes your happiness even greater. And when you face unwanted situations, My Joy gives you the courage and strength to cling to Me and wait for My help. So come to Me, and let Me give you Joy for *all* times.

The Lord has done great things for
us, and we are very glad.
—Psalm 126:3

The everlasting God is your place of safety.
His arms will hold you up forever.
—Deuteronomy 33:27

"You will search for me. And when you search
for me with all your heart, you will find me!"
—Jeremiah 29:13

Now for a short time different kinds of troubles
may make you sad. These troubles come to prove
that your faith is pure. This purity of faith is worth
more than gold. Gold can be proved to be pure by
fire, but gold can be destroyed. But the purity of
your faith will bring you praise and glory and honor
when Jesus Christ comes again. You have not seen
Christ, but still you love him. You cannot see him now,
but you believe in him. You are filled with a joy that
cannot be explained. And that joy is full of glory.
—1 Peter 1:6-8

Perfectly Loved

To truly enjoy your life, you must have hope. But it must be the right kind of hope. A hope that won't let you down.

It's okay to enjoy your stuff, your games and toys. Just don't put your hope in them. They can break or be stolen or simply wear out. And it's okay to enjoy your friends; you need them. But don't put your hope in them either. They'll mess up, make mistakes, and hurt your feelings sometimes.

There is only one kind of hope that will never break, wear out, or let you down. That is the Hope of My Love. My Love is perfect. It never fails. Nothing—*not death, not life, nothing now, nothing in the future—will ever be able to separate you from My Love.*

I watch over those who put their hope in My Love. That doesn't mean you'll never have another problem. It does mean I will always be with you—and you will always be perfectly loved.

The Lord looks after those who fear him. He watches over those who put their hope in his love.

—Psalm 33:18

Yes, I am sure that nothing can separate us from the love God has for us. Not death, not life, not angels, not ruling spirits, nothing now, nothing in the future, no powers, nothing above us, nothing below us, or anything else in the whole world will ever be able to separate us from the love of God that is in Christ Jesus our Lord.

—Romans 8:38–39

We pray that the Lord of peace will give you peace at all times and in every way. May the Lord be with all of you.

—2 Thessalonians 3:16

You Make Me Happy!

You make Me happy! That may be hard for you to believe, but it's true. You make me happy because of the great Love I have for you. I love you more than you can begin to imagine. So relax. Take time to let My Love soak into your heart. And listen while *I sing over you* with joy.

Living in this world is a challenge. There is brokenness all around you—broken people, broken promises, broken things. At times you may be the one who is broken and hurting. Don't let your eyes and your thoughts stay fixed on what is wrong. Choose to focus on Me instead. I'll help you—simply pray, "I want to see You, Jesus."

I died on the cross for you—that's how great My Love is. You don't have to earn My Love. It's simply yours. Live like you *know* that I love you—and that *you* make Me happy!

The Lord your God is with you. The mighty One will save you. The Lord will be happy with you. You will rest in his love. He will sing and be joyful about you.

—ZEPHANIAH 3:17

My heart said of you, "Go, worship him."
So I come to worship you, Lord.

—PSALM 27:8

"May the Lord show you his kindness.
May he have mercy on you. May the Lord
watch over you and give you peace."

—NUMBERS 6:25–26

Because of My Hope . . .

*P*ut *your hope in Me. Praise Me because I am your Savior and God.* Sometimes—especially if you're feeling down—it's hard to keep hoping. When those times come, remember that My kind of hope is much more than just a feeling or a wish.

When snowflakes begin to fall, you might hope—*wish*—for a snow day. This is hoping for something that might *or* might not happen. My kind of hope is *knowing* for absolute certain. What can you know? You can *know* that I am God, your Savior, and I will keep every promise I ever make.

Putting your hope in Me doesn't depend on how you feel. When you're happy, My Hope fills you with even more Joy. And when you're sad, My Hope lifts you out of your sadness with My promise to be with you and take care of you. Because of My Hope, you can always have Joy.

Why am I so sad? Why am I so upset? I should put my hope in God. I should keep praising him, My Savior and my God.

—Psalm 42:5–6

In every way we show that we are servants of God: in accepting many hard things, in troubles, in difficulties, and in great problems. . . . We have much sadness, but we are always rejoicing. We are poor, but we are making many people rich in faith. We have nothing, but really we have everything.

—2 Corinthians 6:4, 10

Through Jesus let us always offer our sacrifice to God. This sacrifice is our praise, coming from lips that speak his name.

—Hebrews 13:15

Shine Like a Star

I am the Light that shines in the darkness. The darkness will never overpower My Light!

When a whole bunch of problems come at you all at once, My Light may seem small. If that happens, stop everything! *Tell Me all your troubles.* I'll help you carry the heavy load, and I'll show you the next step to take. Because no matter how dark this world gets, My Light shines on. And it is *far, far* more powerful than any darkness!

Because you are Mine, My Light shines not only *on* you but *through* you. You *are living with crooked and mean people all around you.* Be kind; be brave; be gentle; show self-control. When you do, you *shine like a star in this dark world.* Spend time with Me. Let Me fill you with My Light so you can shine brightly in the world around you.

The Light shines in the darkness. And the darkness has not overpowered the Light.

—John 1:5

People, trust God all the time. Tell him all your problems. God is our protection.

—Psalm 62:8

Do everything without complaining or arguing. Then you will be innocent and without anything wrong in you. You will be God's children without fault. But you are living with crooked and mean people all around you. Among them you shine like stars in the dark world.

—Philippians 2:14–15

114

A Mystery

Just as the heavens are higher than the earth, so are My ways higher than your ways. People are always trying to make Me smaller. They want a god they can understand and control, who does what *they* want. When that doesn't work, they simply say I'm not real, or they criticize Me.

Sometimes you'll struggle like this too. It's tempting to *depend on your own understanding.* This will never work, because *my thoughts are higher than your thoughts*.

I am the Great Creator. And because I made you in My image, you are a creator too—of stories, of pictures, of things. But you can't create something out of nothing. Only *I* can do that. And I did it when I spoke the world into existence.

When you're struggling to understand Me—to understand why and how—remember who I AM. I am the All-Powerful God. I am a Mystery. But I am a Mystery who loves you and who died to save you.

So you should look for the Lord before it is too late. You should call to him while he is near. . . . The Lord says, "Your thoughts are not like my thoughts. Your ways are not like my ways. Just as the heavens are higher than the earth, so are my ways higher than your ways. And my thoughts are higher than your thoughts."

—Isaiah 55:6, 8–9

Trust the Lord with all your heart. Don't depend on your own understanding.

—Proverbs 3:5

God said, "Let there be light!" And there was light. . . . Then God said, "Let the water under the sky be gathered together so the dry land will appear." And it happened.

—Genesis 1:3, 9

We are told to let
our light shine, and
if it does, we won't
need to tell anybody
it does. Lighthouses
don't fire cannons
to call attention
to their shining—
they just shine.

—D. L. Moody

Yes, God is working in you to help you want to do what pleases him. Then he gives you the power to do it. . . . You will be God's children without fault. But you are living with crooked and mean people all around you. Among them you shine like stars in the dark world.

—Philippians 2:13, 15

Count on Me

I am all around you. I know everything that is happening in your life. I know every thought and feeling. I hear your every prayer. I keep you in *My* thoughts. Now keep Me in *your* thoughts—don't let other things crowd Me out.

Remember that I'm with you every moment of your life. I watch over you with My perfect Love. In fact, *My Love surrounds those who trust in Me.*

I want you to learn to feel My Presence with you—even when friends, family, chores, or struggles demand your attention. I am the One in your life who never changes. I am *the same yesterday, today, and forever.* You can always count on Me.

Keep your eyes and your thoughts on Me. I will show you the right way to go and the right thing to do. As you learn to focus on Me, I bless you with the gift of *My Peace.*

I look up to the hills. But where does my help come from? My help comes from the Lord. He made heaven and earth. He will not let you be defeated. He who guards you never sleeps.

—Psalm 121:1–3

Wicked people have many troubles. But the Lord's love surrounds those who trust him.

—Psalm 32:10

Jesus Christ is the same yesterday, today, and forever.

—Hebrews 13:8

"I leave you peace. My peace I give you. I do not give it to you as the world does. So don't let your hearts be troubled. Don't be afraid."

—John 14:27

Watch and See

I want you to live with Joy. Yes, even when everything is going wrong. When you flunk the test, when you're the last one picked for the team, when your best friend moves away—I *still* want you to have Joy.

At times you'll have struggles. And you'll pray for Me to take them away. Sometimes I will, but sometimes I won't. And when I don't answer your prayers the way you want Me to, you may think you've done something wrong—or that you're somehow missing out on what's best for you. But you're forgetting a most important truth: I am Lord. I am in control, and I am taking care of you.

Depend on Me—with a glad, thankful heart. I won't let you down. *I am good!* Even in difficult times, you can trust that I'm doing the very best thing for you. So *thank Me and praise My Name*. Then just watch and see all the good I will do for you!

Look, the Lord God is coming with power.
He will use his power to rule all the people.
Look, he will bring reward for his people.
He will have their payment with him.

—Isaiah 40:10

You are only human. And human beings
have no right to question God. An object
cannot tell the person who made it,
"Why did you make me like this?"

—Romans 9:20

Come into his city with songs of thanksgiving.
Come into his courtyards with songs of
praise. Thank him, and praise his name. The
Lord is good. His love continues forever.
His loyalty continues from now on.

—Psalm 100:4–5

Your Living God

I am in charge of everything in your life. During the day, *I show you My true Love* with blessings that are too many to count. So be on the lookout for the many gifts I place in your day. That unexpected kind word, that friend who came by at just the right moment, that ray of sunshine that brushed your cheek—those are all from Me. Ask My Spirit to open your eyes to see them. How many can you find?

At night I have a song for you. I sing for you as I lovingly watch over you. When you're lying in bed, waiting to fall asleep, use that time to simply be with Me. Enjoy being still in My Presence. This time together will bring us closer. And as you drift off to sleep, have no fear, because I am watching over you.

Day or night, whether you're awake or asleep, I *am* always with you. For I am *your living God*.

The Lord shows his true love every day. At night I have a song, and I pray to my living God.

—Psalm 42:8

Control yourselves and be careful! The devil is your enemy. And he goes around like a roaring lion looking for someone to eat. Refuse to give in to the devil. Stand strong in your faith. You know that your Christian brothers and sisters all over the world are having the same sufferings you have.

—1 Peter 5:8–9

I remember you while I'm lying in bed. I think about you through the night. You are my help. Because of your protection, I sing. I stay close to you. You support me with your right hand.

—Psalm 63:6–8

118

The Higher You Climb

Climb the mountain of life with Me. Be willing to try new things as I lead you to them. At times the climb will be tough, and you'll get tired. You may look back and wish for the days when things were easier. But those easy times were to train and prepare you for the adventure ahead.

This mountain we're climbing is higher than any you've ever seen—higher even than Mount Everest! Its top is hidden in the clouds, making it impossible for you to know how far you've already climbed—or how far you have left to go. But the higher you climb, the more amazing the view will be!

Although each day will have its challenges, take time to look around you and see the beautiful views. Enjoy My Presence. The higher you climb, the tougher it will be—but your adventure will be that much greater too. And don't forget this either: The higher you climb with Me, the closer you'll be to your goal of heaven!

Six days later, Jesus took Peter, James, and John the brother of James up on a high mountain. They were all alone there. While they watched, Jesus was changed. His face became bright like the sun. And his clothes became white as light.

—Matthew 17:1–2

The Lord God gives me my strength. He makes me like a deer, which does not stumble. He leads me safely on the steep mountains.

—Habakkuk 3:19

Our homeland is in heaven, and we are waiting for our Savior, the Lord Jesus Christ, to come from heaven. He will change our humble bodies and make them like his own glorious body. Christ can do this by his power. With that power he is able to rule all things.

—Philippians 3:20–21

Brighten the Darkness

I will brighten the darkness around you. After all, *I am the Light of the world.* I am with you and within you. Every day, you'll come across dark things in this world—cheating, lies, hurt feelings, and much worse. Sometimes the darkness will be in your own heart—jealousy, anger, or feeling sorry for yourself.

Remember: *I have defeated the world.* You can choose to focus on the dark things or to focus on Me—your Savior who won the greatest victory of all time!

Walk with Me. I'll *guide you down the path to Peace.* This world will try to tug you off My Path. It's your responsibility to keep following Me. You won't do this perfectly all the time, but I'll help you. I'm coaching you to turn your thoughts to Me, in good times and tough times. Stay close to Me, and I'll keep you on the *path to Peace.* I'll *brighten the darkness around you.*

Lord, you give light to my lamp. The Lord
brightens the darkness around me.

—2 Samuel 22:29

"I am the light of the world. The person
who follows me will never live in darkness.
He will have the light that gives life."

—John 8:12

"I told you these things so that you can have
peace in me. In this world you will have trouble.
But be brave! I have defeated the world!"

—John 16:33

"Now you, child, will be called a prophet of the
Most High God. You will go first before the Lord to
prepare the people for his coming. . . . God will help
those who live in darkness, in the fear of death. He
will guide us into the path that goes toward peace."

—Luke 1:76, 79

120

My Master Plan

Lean on Me. *Trust Me with all your heart.* The tougher and more challenging your day is, the more you need to lean on Me.

When problems pop up, it's only natural to depend on yourself, thinking of how you can fix things. But because you're human, your understanding has limits. Your solutions might work sometimes, but other times they might just make a bigger mess! My understanding is unlimited. Let Me help you.

You have every reason to trust Me. After all, I created the entire universe, and I keep it all going. Someday I will bring all those who love Me to heaven. I *can* take care of you.

Be brave! Lean on Me in this broken world. Believe that My plan for you is working—through the good times and the bad. Your troubles are part of My perfect Master Plan. You will learn and grow from them. And they will one day bring you *an eternal glory* that will be *much greater* than any trouble you have right now!

Trust the Lord with all your heart. Don't depend on your own understanding.

—Proverbs 3:5

God is the One who made all things. And all things are for his glory. . . . So God made perfect the One who leads people to salvation. He made Jesus a perfect Savior through Jesus' suffering.

—Hebrews 2:10

We have small troubles for a while now, but they are helping us gain an eternal glory. That glory is much greater than the troubles.

—2 Corinthians 4:17

God loves
each of us
as if there
were only
one of us.

—AUGUSTINE

[Jesus] is always able to save those who come to God through him. He can do this, because he always lives, ready to help those who come before God.

—HEBREWS 7:25

Be Still and Know

Be still, and know that I am God. Your life can get crazy sometimes. As you grow up, there are lots of changes and new responsibilities. You still try to spend time alone with Me, but it gets harder and harder to really *be still* and think only about Me. Keep trying—it's so very important.

Decide on a time that will be just for Me. Turn off all the noises—the TV, your computer, your phone. Find a quiet place and then listen to Me—with your Bible open. I am the Bread of Life. Without Me, your soul will starve. Other people may not notice, but *you* will know.

As you quiet yourself and listen to Me, feel My delight in you. I see you as the beloved person you truly are. Open your arms and your heart to Me. The Light of My Love is shining upon you. Let it warm you and strengthen you as you remember *that I am God.*

God says, "Be still and know that I am God. I will be praised in all the nations. I will be praised throughout the earth."

—Psalm 46:10

There are godly people in the world. I enjoy them.

—Psalm 16:3

The Lord makes me very happy. All that I am rejoices in my God. The Lord has covered me with clothes of salvation. He has covered me with a coat of goodness. I am like a bridegroom dressed for his wedding. I am like a bride dressed in jewels.

—Isaiah 61:10

You keep your loving promise. You lead the people you have saved. With your strength you will guide them to your holy land.

—Exodus 15:13

A Hiding Place

Do you have a good hiding place? A secret spot where you go to hide away from the world for a little while? Perhaps it's in your room, a corner of the family room, or even up in the branches of a backyard tree. At times, you just need to get away from the world and all its mess. You need a *refuge*—a safe place to hide. *I* want to be that place for you.

I am good—100 percent good! *I protect you in times of trouble.* I care for you. *I am Light, and in Me there is no darkness at all.* Look for Me, especially in times of trouble.

When you're hurting, I'll wrap you up in My arms. I'll shelter you in My Presence. Count on Me. I promise that *I will be with you always*. Trust in Me, and I will take care of you.

The Lord is good. He gives protection in times
of trouble. He knows who trusts in him.

—Nahum 1:7

Here is the message we have heard from
God and now tell to you: God is light, and
in him there is no darkness at all.

—1 John 1:5

When I am afraid, I will trust you.

—Psalm 56:3

"Go and make followers of all people in the
world. Baptize them in the name of the Father
and the Son and the Holy Spirit. Teach them to
obey everything that I have told you. You can
be sure that I will be with you always. I will
continue with you until the end of the world."

—Matthew 28:19–20

Because of Me

Through My Power all things were made—things on heaven and on earth, things seen and unseen. I am your Creator as well as your Savior.

Every breath you take is a gift from Me. So begin each day by thanking Me for the precious gift of life. Thank Me when you wake up smiling and happy. And thank Me even when you wake up feeling yucky, grouchy, or sad. Starting your day with thanksgiving helps you remember that I am God—and it helps you follow Me through the rest of your day.

All things continue because of Me. This world keeps spinning because of Me. The sun rises and sets and the seasons change because of Me. So put Me first in your life. Bring all your thoughts and plans to Me. Ask Me to show you the way. Because I am the One who keeps all things going, your life will go so much better when there is more of Me in it!

Through his power all things were made—things
in heaven and on earth, things seen and unseen,
all powers, authorities, lords, and rulers. All
things were made through Christ and for Christ.
Christ was there before anything was made.
And all things continue because of him.

—Colossians 1:16–17

The Lord says, "I will make you wise. I will show you
where to go. I will guide you and watch over you."

—Psalm 32:8

Tell me in the morning about your love.
I trust you. Show me what I should do
because my prayers go up to you.

—Psalm 143:8

124

While You Wait

*Y*ou can be happy because of the hope you have of sharing in My Glory. Lots of people use the word *hope* to mean wishful thinking. But My Hope is more than a wish; it's absolute Truth. I have promised that My children will share My Glory in heaven. I *will* keep that promise. And I have all the Power I need to do it!

Hope is for something that will happen in the future; it has not yet happened. So you'll have to wait patiently until I finish keeping My promises. That can be hard, but remember that patience is a *fruit of the Spirit*. You can ask the Holy Spirit to help you wait.

Waiting can sometimes be boring—but not when you're waiting with Me! I fill your day with gifts, blessings, and delights. I am the Creator of everything—stars and starfish, mountains and mountain lions, winds and weather. Enjoy this awesome adventure of being with *Me*—today, tomorrow, and forever!

We have been made right with God because of our faith. So we have peace with God through our Lord Jesus Christ. Through our faith, Christ has brought us into that blessing of God's grace that we now enjoy. And we are happy because of the hope we have of sharing God's glory.

—Romans 5:1–2

We have sufferings now. But the sufferings we have now are nothing compared to the great glory that will be given to us.

—Romans 8:18

The Spirit gives love, joy, peace, patience, kindness, goodness, faithfulness, gentleness, self-control. There is no law that says these things are wrong.

—Galatians 5:22–23

With a Thankful Heart

Come to Me with songs of thanksgiving and *songs of praise.* These are the gifts I want from you.

You have so many blessings in your life that sometimes you take them for granted. You may start to see only the things you *don't* have, instead of all the things you *do* have—and then you miss My Joy completely.

I love it when you praise Me on good days, but I especially treasure your praises when you're having a terrible day. Why? Because I know that on those days, you've searched hard to find Me and My blessings.

Stop now for a just a moment, and take a look around you. How many good things from Me do you see? A beautiful world to live in, air to breathe, people who love you, and—most wonderful of all—a Savior who loves you so much that He died to save you. *Give thanks to Me for My Love*, and *tell others—with Joy—what I have done.*

Come into his city with songs of thanksgiving.
Come into his courtyards with songs of
praise. Thank him, and praise his name. The
Lord is good. His love continues forever.
His loyalty continues from now on.

—Psalm 100:4–5

Let them give thanks to the Lord for his love
and for the miracles he does for people.
Let them offer sacrifices to thank him. With
joy they should tell what he has done.

—Psalm 107:21–22

"Now you are sad. But I will see you again and you
will be happy. And no one will take away your joy."

—John 16:22

The Comfort of My Love

What are the things that comfort you? A soft blanket, a warm hug from your mom or dad, a faithful pet to cuddle with? The things that comfort you are the things you can depend on. My Love is like that, only much better! You can *always* rely on it—it never fails, never ends.

There is never a time when I am *not* with you. But in order to feel the comfort of My Presence, you must trust Me with all your heart. Then I'll not only give you comfort, but I'll also give you strength. My comfort—and My Love—will give you strength to do whatever I ask of you.

When you need comfort, come to Me. Let Me *comfort you with My Love*. Take time to enjoy My Presence. Listen as I sing of My great Love for you. It is greater than you could ever imagine—and it is *a Love that will last forever*.

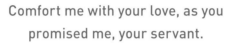

Comfort me with your love, as you
promised me, your servant.

—Psalm 119:76

The Lord your God is with you. The mighty One will
save you. The Lord will be happy with you. You will
rest in his love. He will sing and be joyful about you.

—Zephaniah 3:17

The Lord appeared to his people. He said, "I love you
people with a love that will last forever. I became
your friend because of my love and kindness."

—Jeremiah 31:3

Hope is
one of
the principal
springs that
keep mankind
in motion.

—THOMAS FULLER

So, Lord,
what hope
do I have?
You are
my hope.

—Psalm 39:7

Much More than a Hero!

I am God your Savior. If I were only a human hero, I couldn't save you from your sins or give you never-ending Love or offer you heaven. But I am much, much more than just a human hero. I am your All-Powerful God!

But if I had stayed *only* God, I couldn't have been your Savior. I had to become human for a time, die on the cross, and be raised to life again—so that I could defeat sin and death. Because I became human, I can save you from your sins and give you never-ending Love and offer you the promise of heaven.

Look for Me—I am with you in every moment. I always hear your prayers. And I am always working in your life. *I made you and I will take care of you. I will carry you, and I will save you.* I am God your Savior!

I will look to the Lord for help. I will wait for God to save me. My God will hear me.

—MICAH 7:7

The Spirit helps us. We are very weak, but the Spirit helps us with our weakness. We do not know how to pray as we should. But the Spirit himself speaks to God for us, even begs God for us. The Spirit speaks to God with deep feelings that words cannot explain.

—ROMANS 8:26

"Even when you are old, I will take care of you. Even when your hair has turned gray, I will take care of you. I made you and will take care of you. I will carry you, and I will save you."

—ISAIAH 46:4

128

When You Feel Weak

This world thinks that feeling tired and weak is a bad thing. People spend all kinds of time and money on exercise machines, fitness classes, and vitamins for their bodies. None of those things is wrong, but don't forget that your greatest source of strength and energy is . . . *Me.*

Feeling weak and tired isn't a bad thing. It's simply part of living in this world. Bring your tiredness to Me. I lived as a human in this world for thirty-three years. I understand how it feels.

Maybe you're tired of troubles or tired of trying to do the right thing—and still having it turn out wrong. Maybe you're weak from too many struggles or from illness or worry. Come to Me and tell Me everything.

Spend time with Me. Feel the warmth of My Love. As My Love shines on you, I will bless you. *I give strength to those who are tired. I give more power to those who are weak.*

The Lord gives strength to those who are tired. He gives more power to those who are weak. Even boys become tired and need to rest. Even young men trip and fall. But the people who trust the Lord will become strong again. They will be able to rise up as an eagle in the sky. They will run without needing rest. They will walk without becoming tired.

—Isaiah 40:29–31

May the Lord show you his kindness.
May he have mercy on you. May the Lord
watch over you and give you peace.

—Numbers 6:25–26

Show your kindness to me, your servant.
Save me because of your love.

—Psalm 31:16

The All-Powerful God

This planet that you live on is a big mess. Just listening to the news can make you worry. Wars and crime and terrible things seem to be out of control.

That's why it's so important to remember who I am: *I am the One who is and was and is coming.* I am the Creator of time. I know everything about the beginning of this world—its story. And I know every detail about the rest of the story.

I am the All-Powerful God! I not only know what will happen, but I am in control. The more helpless you feel, the more important it is to believe that I have complete Power to do anything that needs to be done.

And I love you. I am the Lord who *comforts His people.* You can rise above the troubles of this world because I am both mighty and loving. So you have good reason to *be happy*; sometimes you may even *shout with Joy*!

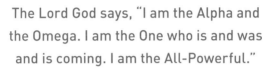

The Lord God says, "I am the Alpha and
the Omega. I am the One who is and was
and is coming. I am the All-Powerful."

—Revelation 1:8

Those who go to God Most High for safety will
be protected by God All-Powerful. I will say
to the Lord, "You are my place of safety and
protection. You are my God, and I trust you."

—Psalm 91:1–2

Heavens and earth, be happy. Mountains, shout
with joy. Be happy because the Lord comforts
his people. He will comfort those who suffer.

—Isaiah 49:13

Pray Big!

What can you imagine? How big can you dream? Now listen to this: *I can do much, much more than anything you could ever ask or think of.* So don't pray small—pray big!

I am always working in your life, even when you don't see anything happening. You can only see this present moment, so you can't know all that's really going on. But I can see the big picture—all the moments of your life—and I am doing more than you could ever dream!

Talk to Me as you go through your day. Start first thing in the morning—that makes it easier to keep talking to Me all day long. Tell Me everything, because I understand you perfectly. Bring Me your praises, your problems, and your requests. Pray big! And you'll begin to see how I really can do far *more than you could ever ask or think of.*

With God's power working in us, God can do much,
much more than anything we can ask or think of.

—Ephesians 3:20

The Lord is king. He is clothed with majesty.
The Lord is clothed with majesty and armed
with strength. The world is set, and it
cannot be moved. Lord, your kingdom was
set up long ago. You are everlasting.

—Psalm 93:1–2

Lord, every morning you hear my
voice. Every morning, I tell you what I
need. And I wait for your answer.

—Psalm 5:3

131

The Courage to Hope

Hope and courage are like partners in a beautiful dance—they work better together.

When you are waiting . . . and waiting . . . and waiting for the answer to a prayer, it takes courage to keep hoping, trusting, and believing that I will answer. It would be much easier to simply give up. But giving up will only hurt you in the end. So be brave! Choose to keep hoping in Me—and praying to Me!

The word *courage* actually comes from the French word for "heart." Because I live in your heart, you can call upon Me to give you courage. I'll help you face worry, fear, even danger—with confidence.

I know exactly what you're going through, and I love helping you—so let Me! Don't give up. Refuse to give in. I will be here for you—especially when you are bravely *trusting in My Love.* I will give you the courage to hope.

Be strong and brave. Don't be afraid of them.
Don't be frightened. The Lord your God will go
with you. He will not leave you or forget you.
—Deuteronomy 31:6

I pray that you will have greater understanding in
your heart. Then you will know the hope that God
has chosen to give us. I pray that you will know
that the blessings God has promised his holy
people are rich and glorious. And you will know
that God's power is very great for us who believe.
—Ephesians 1:18–19

The Lord is pleased with those who fear
him, with those who trust his love.
—Psalm 147:11

Part of My Family

*Y*ou are holy—*without blame before Me.* You may not completely understand these words right now—but they are some of the most important ones you'll ever read. This means that when you choose to follow Me, you belong to Me. I make you *holy* and *without blame.*

You mess up every day. Everyone does. On your own, you can never be holy or perfect or without sin. But when you trust Me as your Savior, you give Me all your sins—yesterday's, today's, and all of tomorrow's. I take those sins away, and I give you My holiness. You become part of My family.

I paid a terrible price on the cross for this blessing. But I did it because I love you. Take time to think about *how wide and how long and how high and how deep is this huge ocean of Love I have for you. My Love is greater than you could ever know.*

In Christ, he chose us before the world was made. In his love he chose us to be his holy people—people without blame before him.

—Ephesians 1:4

In Christ we are set free by the blood of his death. And so we have forgiveness of sins because of God's rich grace.

—Ephesians 1:7

I pray that Christ will live in your hearts because of your faith. I pray that your life will be strong in love and be built on love. And I pray that you and all God's holy people will have the power to understand the greatness of Christ's love. I pray that you can understand how wide and how long and how high and how deep that love is. Christ's love is greater than any person can ever know. But I pray that you will be able to know that love. Then you can be filled with the fullness of God.

—Ephesians 3:17–19

Some people think
God does not like
to be troubled with
our constant coming
and asking. The way
to trouble God is
not to come at all.

—D. L. MOODY

Through his glory and goodness, he gave us the very great and rich gifts he promised us. With those gifts you can share in God's nature. And so the world will not ruin you with its evil desires.

—2 Peter 1:4

Words of Hope

Sometimes your life can feel like an out-of-control roller coaster—and all you can do is hold on! Make sure you're holding on to *Me*.

I know you're smart. You're growing up, and you want to figure things out for yourself. But this isn't always possible. The best thing to do is come to Me and tell Me you trust Me. Say it out loud: "Jesus, I trust You!" Your words of hope make a difference, not only to other people but to you. They give you strength and courage.

Trusting Me will give you courage because you *know* that I keep My promises. *I will not let you go through anything more than you can stand.* I'll give you *a way to escape.* Sometimes that way will be through your own words, especially your prayers. You can pray: "Jesus, You are my Hope!" Simple prayers like this will help you *hold on firmly to your hope.*

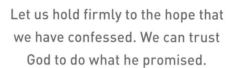

Let us hold firmly to the hope that
we have confessed. We can trust
God to do what he promised.

—Hebrews 10:23

Lord, hear me when I call. Be kind and
answer me. My heart said of you, "Go, worship
him." So I come to worship you, Lord.

—Psalm 27:7–8

The only temptations that you have are the
temptations that all people have. But you can
trust God. He will not let you be tempted more
than you can stand. But when you are tempted,
God will also give you a way to escape that
temptation. Then you will be able to stand it.

—1 Corinthians 10:13

134

Who You Are

Do you ever feel small? Unimportant? Too young? That is *not* the plan that I have for you! *I came to give you Life—Life in all its fullness.*

I want you to live fully each and every day of this adventure. To do this, you must remember who you are and Who you belong to—Me! You are My beloved one. You have been adopted into the family of God. You are not a guest or visitor—you are a forever member of My family.

Don't let this truth become ordinary to you. Let it always amaze and inspire you. You are *Mine*! Stay close to Me. That way, you won't miss one second of the grand adventure that you are on with Me.

When you live in My Presence, you and your choices *will* make a difference in this world—no matter how old you are. And *I will guide you from now on, forever and ever.*

So Jesus said again, "I tell you the truth. I am the door for the sheep. All the people who came before me were thieves and robbers. The sheep did not listen to them. I am the door. The person who enters through me will be saved. He will be able to come in and go out and find pasture. A thief comes to steal and kill and destroy. But I came to give life—life in all its fullness."

—JOHN 10:7–10

The Spirit himself joins with our spirits
to say that we are God's children.

—ROMANS 8:16

This God is our God forever and ever.
He will guide us from now on.

—PSALM 48:14

Small Troubles?

The apostle Paul called his troubles "small." The word he used means they weigh almost nothing. But he was beaten with rods three times, hit with a whip five times, and once he was even stoned. He was shipwrecked three times and spent a day and a night in the sea. He was often hungry, thirsty, and cold. Yet Paul said his enormous troubles were *small*—light as a feather. How could that be?

Paul could say this because he was comparing his troubles with *eternal Glory*. So even though some of his experiences were terrible, they were like the blink of an eye compared to the Joy of Jesus—which lasts forever and ever.

I want you to see your troubles—the big ones and the small ones—the same way Paul did. Trust Me to use your troubles to teach you important lessons here and now. I'll also use them to build up rewards for you in heaven.

So trust Me—Your troubles won't last forever, but My Love and Joy and Salvation will!

We have small troubles for a while now, but they are helping us gain an eternal glory. That glory is much greater than the troubles.

—2 Corinthians 4:17

Five times the Jews have given me their punishment of 39 lashes with a whip. Three different times I was beaten with rods. One time they tried to kill me with stones. Three times I was in ships that were wrecked, and one of those times I spent the night and the next day in the sea. I have gone on many travels. And I have been in danger from rivers, from thieves, from my own people, the Jews, and from those who are not Jews. I have been in danger in cities, in places where no one lives, and on the sea. And I have been in danger with false brothers. I have done hard and tiring work, and many times I did not sleep. I have been hungry and thirsty. Many times I have been without food. I have been cold and without clothes.

—2 Corinthians 11:24–27

Choosing What to Do

Basketball, soccer, and band. Quiet time, homework, and chores. Movies with friends, family time, and youth group retreats. Even though you're young, there's so much to do!

The fact is, you won't be able to do all the things you want to do—or even all the things other people want you to do (though you need to obey Mom and Dad). Your time and energy are limited. So before you choose your activities, say a prayer and I will show you what's truly important.

Checking with Me—with My Word—will help you make the best use of your time. It will also take away worries or guilt about the choices you make.

When you let Me be your Guide, you can relax and focus on doing well at the things I consider important. And as you do what pleases Me, you'll grow more and more like the masterpiece I created you to be.

Depend on the Lord and his strength.
Always go to him for help.

—Psalm 105:4

Your promises are so sweet to me. They are
like honey to my mouth! Your orders give me
understanding. So I hate lying ways. Your word is
like a lamp for my feet and a light for my way.

—Psalm 119:103–105

God has made us what we are. In Christ
Jesus, God made us new people so that we
would do good works. God had planned in
advance those good works for us. He had
planned for us to live our lives doing them.

—Ephesians 2:10

A Wide-Open Space

How do you feel in a big crowd, when people are so tightly packed together that it's hard to move? It can be scary—and make you wish for a wide-open space. Sometimes your life can feel like that: crowded with things to do, with stuff, with worry and fear.

When you feel cramped in life, I will bring you out into *a safe place. I will save you* because *you delight Me.* What is that safe place? It is the wide-openness of salvation. When you follow Me, My Spirit comes to live inside you. He creates space in your heart and soul—space for Me.

One day, that safe, wonderfully open place will be heaven. I will *wipe away every tear. There will be no more death, sadness, crying, or pain.* My Love will wash over you like the waves of the ocean. And you will finally be able to love Me—and everyone—with perfect Love!

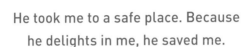

He took me to a safe place. Because
he delights in me, he saved me.
—2 Samuel 22:20

You guide me with your advice. And
later you will receive me in honor.
—Psalm 73:24

I heard a loud voice from the throne. The voice
said, "Now God's home is with men. He will
live with them, and they will be his people.
God himself will be with them and will be their
God. He will wipe away every tear from their
eyes. There will be no more death, sadness,
crying, or pain. All the old ways are gone."
—Revelation 21:3–4

All Day Long

I am *your God* and *your Savior*. I will *guide* you and teach you. Put your hope in Me, and *trust Me all day long*.

The *all day long* part is important. It's not as hard to trust Me when you're feeling good and things are going smoothly. But when you're tired, or things get too busy or difficult, you may forget about Me. Yet this is when you need Me the most! Because I am both your Savior and your God, I am able to help you through any troubles or struggles that come your way.

Make it your goal to keep Me in your thoughts *all day long*. I understand that you won't be able to do this perfectly, but it's a wonderful goal to have. It will help you control what you're thinking. And it will help you see and enjoy My Presence as we travel along together.

Guide me in your truth. Teach me, my God,
my Savior. I trust you all day long.

—Psalm 25:5

You will have many kinds of troubles. But when
these things happen, you should be very happy.

—James 1:2

I keep the Lord before me always. Because he is
close by my side I will not be hurt. So I rejoice, and I
am glad. Even my body has hope. . . . You will teach
me God's way to live. Being with you will fill me with
joy. At your right hand I will find pleasure forever.

—Psalm 16:8–9, 11

The future
is as
bright
as the
promises
of God.

—ADONIRAM JUDSON

The way of
the good
person is like
the light of dawn.
It grows brighter
and brighter until
it is full daylight.

—Proverbs 4:18

The Greatest Catcher

I am the greatest Catcher of all time! But you might be surprised by what I catch. It's not balls; it's not fish. I catch worries, fears, and doubts. So throw *all your worries to Me*. Why? Because *I am guarding you* and watching over you, prepared to receive your burdens from you.

Don't hesitate—throw all your worries to Me. As soon as you give Me those heavy loads of fear, doubt, and concern, you can breathe a sigh of relief. You may have to do this many times a day—and even at night. That's just fine! I'm always awake and ready to catch your troubles. No matter how much you throw at Me, I *never* miss!

Because I am All-Powerful, carrying your burdens doesn't make Me tired. In fact, I enjoy this game of catch because I see your load becoming lighter and your face becoming brighter.

Don't let your worries and fears weigh you down. Instead, look to Me with a smile and say, "Catch, Jesus!" Then throw them into My waiting hands.

Give all your worries to him,
because he cares for you.
—1 Peter 5:7

God, examine me and know my heart.
Test me and know my thoughts.
—Psalm 139:23

The sun cannot hurt you during the day. And
the moon cannot hurt you at night. The Lord
will guard you from all dangers. He will
guard your life. The Lord will guard you as
you come and go, both now and forever.
—Psalm 121:6–8

Praise the Lord, day by day. God our Savior helps us.
—Psalm 68:19

One Step at a Time

Sometimes the journey of your life can make you really tired. Some days will feel like you've walked a mile uphill in July, wearing your heaviest coat! You just don't want to take another step. When those times come, take a moment and remember Me.

Remember that I am always walking with you. Lean on Me. I am eager to help you take that next step—and then the one after that. There's no need to worry about what might be miles down the road. After all, you can only take one step at a time.

Don't look at your future with a frown, dreading the days ahead of you. It may be difficult, but I am right beside you. Keep talking to Me and trusting Me. When you look at Me through eyes of faith, the bright hope of heaven shines on you and your path, lighting up the way just before you.

"Come to me, all of you who are tired and
have heavy loads. I will give you rest."
—Matthew 11:28

We were saved, and we have this hope. If we see
what we are waiting for, then that is not really hope.
People do not hope for something they already
have. But we are hoping for something that we
do not have yet. We are waiting for it patiently.
—Romans 8:24–25

The Lord will save me when anyone tries
to hurt me. The Lord will bring me safely
to his heavenly kingdom. Glory forever
and ever be the Lord's. Amen.
—2 Timothy 4:18

Happy are the people who know how to praise you.
Lord, let them live in the light of your presence.
—Psalm 89:15

Leave Room for Mystery

A *mystery* is something you don't understand. And this world is filled with mysteries—like how each snowflake is different from every other, or how the wind knows which way to blow.

My ways are often a mystery to you—like why bad things happen to good people, or good things happen to bad people. You wish you could always know what I'm thinking, but your knowledge only goes so far.

Leave room for mystery in your thoughts about Me. You can never completely understand Me, control Me, or predict what I will do. But you can always trust Me and believe that I will do the very best thing for you. Learn to enjoy the wonders of Me rather than worrying about the mysteries of Me.

I know how each snowflake is made. *I* tell the winds where to blow. When there is something you can't make sense of, trust Me—and trust that there are some *things too wonderful for you to know.*

Without doubt, the secret of our life of worship
is great: He was shown to us in a human body,
proved right by the Spirit, and seen by angels.
He was preached to the nations, believed in
by the world, and taken to heaven in glory.
—1 Timothy 3:16

Then [Job] bowed down to the ground to worship
God. He said: "I was naked when I was born.
And I will be naked when I die. The Lord gave
these things to me. And he has taken them
away. Praise the name of the Lord." In all
this Job did not sin. He did not blame God.
—Job 1:20–22

You asked, "Who is this that made my purpose
unclear by saying things that are not true?"
Surely I talked about things I did not understand.
I spoke of things too wonderful for me to know.
—Job 42:3

Close as a Whisper

I am as close as a whispered prayer.

People who love one another want to be close. Your mom may hug you tight and whisper sweet nicknames. Your dad may tuck you in with a quiet "I love you." I want to be close to you like that. I want to whisper tender words of My Love to you.

I am close to everyone who prays to Me. I hear even your softest prayer. This is My promise to all My loved ones.

Of course, I answer silent prayers, but whispering the words can help you feel closer to Me. Hearing your own voice call to Me will make you more aware of My unseen Presence. And I will answer you. I rarely speak in a voice you could hear with your ears. But you can hear My voice whispering in your heart. Hear Me saying, "I am with you. I love you. *I will never leave you alone.*"

The Lord is close to everyone who prays
to him, to all who truly pray to him.
—Psalm 145:18

"Just as I was with Moses, so I will be with you.
No one will be able to stop you all your life. I will
not leave you. I will never leave you alone."
—Joshua 1:5

The Lord said to Elijah, "Go. Stand in front of me
on the mountain. I will pass by you." Then a very
strong wind blew. It caused the mountains to
break apart. It broke apart large rocks in front of
the Lord. But the Lord was not in the wind. After
the wind, there was an earthquake. But the Lord
was not in the earthquake. After the earthquake,
there was a fire. But the Lord was not in the fire.
After the fire, there was a quiet, gentle voice.
—1 Kings 19:11–12

Stop, Look, and Listen

Stop, look, and listen—you've probably heard this little saying about the safe way to cross a street. But it's also a good reminder for your journey through life with Me.

When you start your day, *stop* for a moment to talk to Me. *Look* at all the proof of My Presence in your life. And *listen* for what I want to say to you this day.

On happy days, *stop* to praise Me. *Look* at My many blessings. *Listen* to how much I love you. When you're having a hard day or facing a tough decision, *stop* to tell Me all about it. *Look* for the ways I'm already helping you. *Listen* as My Spirit tells your heart the next step to take. Then *stop*, *look*, and *listen* again.

As you practice doing this, you'll become more and more aware of Me working in your life. You'll feel more alive and more filled with Joy—the more you stop, look, and listen.

Be glad that you are his. Let those who ask the Lord for help be happy.

—Psalm 105:3

"My sheep listen to my voice. I know them, and they follow me. I give them eternal life, and they will never die. And no person can steal them out of my hand."

—John 10:27–28

Then a cloud appeared and enveloped them, and a voice came from the cloud: "This is my Son, whom I love. Listen to him!"

—Mark 9:7 NIV

Pray in the Spirit at all times. Pray with all kinds of prayers, and ask for everything you need. To do this you must always be ready. Never give up. Always pray for all God's people.

—Ephesians 6:18

The Battle for Self-Control

Self-control means . . . controlling yourself. That sounds simple enough, but it can be oh-so-hard to do. Like when you're angry or tired or jealous or feeling selfish. Sometimes self-control can be a battle.

But you don't have to fight this battle alone. My Spirit, who lives within you, is your Helper. And part of *the fruit of the Spirit is . . . self-control.* It's not good to fight without protection. *Wear faith and love to protect you. And the hope of salvation should be your helmet.*

Armor is designed to protect your heart and other important organs when you are in battle. *Faith, hope, and love* all work together to shield you. Your faith in Me helps you keep trusting Me—even in tough times. Love is the reason I saved you. And *the hope of salvation* makes a wonderful helmet because it protects your mind and reminds you that you belong to Me—forever!

We belong to the day; so we should control
ourselves. We should wear faith and love to protect
us. And the hope of salvation should be our helmet.

—1 Thessalonians 5:8

The Spirit gives love, joy, peace, patience, kindness,
goodness, faithfulness, gentleness, self-control.
There is no law that says these things are wrong.

—Galatians 5:22–23

So stand strong, with the belt of truth tied around
your waist. And on your chest wear the protection
of right living. And on your feet wear the Good
News of peace to help you stand strong.

—Ephesians 6:14–15

So these three things continue forever: faith,
hope and love. And the greatest of these is love.

—1 Corinthians 13:13

When you remember that the road we're traveling on is really a highway to heaven, the roughness or smoothness of the road becomes less important to you. I am training you to keep your focus on My Presence with you *and* the hope of heaven.

—*Jesus Calling: 365 Devotions for Kids*

Prepare your minds
for service and have
self-control. All
your hope should
be for the gift of
grace that will be
yours when Jesus
Christ comes again.

—1 Peter 1:13

Live Bravely!

I want you to face this world with courage and confidence. I know you're young, so that probably sounds like a lot to ask. But I am with you. My Spirit lives in you. You have everything you need to *be strong and brave*, so *put your hope in Me*.

Fear and cowardice are not from Me. When you start to feel you can't handle whatever is happening, remember who you are: a child of the eternal King! Ask Me to help you with your troubles. Let the Light of My Presence make you strong. When you live bravely, encouraged by My promises, I am pleased.

But what is *living bravely*? It is doing what is right *even* when no one else is. It is sticking up for those who can't stick up for themselves. It is helping and serving others. It is telling the world about Me—even if people make fun of you.

When you try to live bravely, I make you even stronger and *more* courageous!

All you who put your hope in the
Lord be strong and brave.

—Psalm 31:24

The Spirit that we received is not a spirit that
makes us slaves again to fear. The Spirit that we
have makes us children of God. And with that
Spirit we say, "Father, dear Father." And the Spirit
himself joins with our spirits to say that we are
God's children. If we are God's children, then we
will receive the blessings God has for us.

—Romans 8:15–17

Honor and glory to the King that rules forever! He
cannot be destroyed and cannot be seen. Honor
and glory forever and ever to the only God. Amen.

—1 Timothy 1:17

Christ is faithful as a Son who is the head of God's
family. And we are God's family if we hold on to our
faith and are proud of the great hope we have.

—Hebrews 3:6

At the End of the Day

When you've had a tiring day, a soft pillow feels so soothing. You can just sink down into it and rest. My Peace is like a comfortable pillow at the end of a long day—soft and soothing. When you lie down at night, let all your worries and your plans for tomorrow drift away. Sink down in My Peace and rest.

Whisper, "I trust You, Jesus." There's no need to fear. You are safe in the protection of My Presence. If any worries try to creep into your mind, give them to Me. And then thank Me because I know and understand everything about you. I love you, and I'll take care of you. Think about these precious truths instead of your problems.

While you're resting, I am not. I'm already at work in your tomorrow, smoothing out your path through the day and preparing everything you need. I am All-Powerful, All-Knowing, and I never leave you alone in your hard times! So let go of worries, relax—and rest in My Peace.

The Lord answered, "I myself will go
with you. And I will give you victory."
—Exodus 33:14

Be full of joy in the Lord always. I will say again,
be full of joy. Let all men see that you are gentle
and kind. The Lord is coming soon. Do not
worry about anything. But pray and ask God for
everything you need. And when you pray, always
give thanks. And God's peace will keep your hearts
and minds in Christ Jesus. The peace that God
gives is so great that we cannot understand it.
—Philippians 4:4–7

Jesus said to the Jews who believed in him,
"If you continue to obey my teaching, you are
truly my followers. Then you will know the
truth. And the truth will make you free."
—John 8:31–32

147

Waiting for Sleep

In this world, you will have to wait. You'll wait in line; you'll wait for your birthday; you'll wait for your turn. But one of the hardest times to wait is when you can't fall asleep at night. You keep expecting sleep to come—but it just doesn't.

Maybe something wonderful is happening tomorrow, and you can't sleep because you're so excited. Or maybe your body is too tired and too achy to rest. Or maybe there's something worrying you or frightening you. The darkness seems so dark and scary, you can't wait for the sun to rise again.

When the night goes on too long and you're looking for the light of day, remember that I am with you. *I will be your Light.* Rest in Me. I'll watch over you until the morning comes. And then . . . I'll still be with you. *Wait for Me to help you.*

I wait for the Lord to help me. I trust his word. I wait for the Lord to help me more than night watchmen wait for the dawn, more than night watchmen wait for the dawn.

—PSALM 130:5–6

Because I have lived right, I will see your face. When I wake up, I will see your likeness and be satisfied.

—PSALM 17:15

With God's power working in us, God can do much, much more than anything we can ask or think of.

—EPHESIANS 3:20

The sun will no longer be your light during the day. The light from the moon will no longer be your light. This is because the Lord will be your light forever. Your God will be your glory.

—ISAIAH 60:19

148

My Word Is Alive

My Word is alive and working. Because the words of the Bible are alive and full of Power, they can touch your heart and change your life. Reading My Word causes you to be more like Me. And the more of My Word you have in your mind and heart, the more I can shape you.

Growing up is about much more than just growing taller. It is about growing spiritually stronger and becoming more like Me. This will mean *a lot* of changes! Some of those changes will be easy and pleasant—like loving those who love you or singing My praises on happy days. Some of them will be harder and not-so-fun—like loving your enemies and praising Me on sad days.

Keep trusting Me, though, and holding on to My hand. I'm working to make you all I created you to be. Keep reading My Word. Memorize verses from it, for *My Word is like a lamp for your feet and a light for your way.*

God's word is alive and working. It is sharper than a sword sharpened on both sides. It cuts all the way into us, where the soul and the spirit are joined. It cuts to the center of our joints and our bones. And God's word judges the thoughts and feelings in our hearts.

—Hebrews 4:12

Jesus Christ is the same yesterday, today, and forever.

—Hebrews 13:8

God knew them before he made the world. And God chose them to be like his Son. Then Jesus would be the firstborn of many brothers.

—Romans 8:29

Your word is like a lamp for my feet and a light for my way.

—Psalm 119:105

Either Way, You Win!

Some problems come and go . . . and then come back again! When that happens, you may start to worry about when they might come back *yet again*. You may wake up in the morning, scared that this could be the day. This is not a good way to start your day! You're already afraid it's going to be a bad day—before you even get out of bed.

Let Me tell you about a better way: If the problem is *not* there when you wake up, be happy. Thank Me every time you remember that it isn't there. And if the problem *is* there, say, "I trust You with this, Jesus." Ask My Spirit to help you get through it. Keep talking to Me and trusting Me. Then thank Me—and be happy anyway—because I am with you.

Either way, you win! So *be happy. Never stop praying. Give thanks whatever happens.* Because you are with Me, and I am with you.

Be joyful because you have hope. Be patient when trouble comes. Pray at all times.

—Romans 12:12

Always be happy. Never stop praying. Give thanks whatever happens. That is what God wants for you in Christ Jesus.

—1 Thessalonians 5:16–18

Tell me in the morning about your love. I trust you. Show me what I should do because my prayers go up to you.

—Psalm 143:8

I Live in You!

I am the Messiah—the Savior of the world—and I live in *you*!
This is My promise to all who follow Me: *I will live in your hearts because of your faith.* The more you trust Me, the more My Spirit will bless you and the more I will live through you.

I am your only hope for glory. I am the only way to heaven. When you trust Me as your Savior, the promise of living forever in heaven with Me is like a Light—a Light so bright that some of its rays shine on you even now!

I am *the Light that shines in the darkness.* As you follow Me along the path of your life—staying close to Me—this Light *will grow brighter and brighter.*

God decided to let his people know this rich and glorious truth which he has for all people. This truth is Christ himself, who is in you. He is our only hope for glory.

—Colossians 1:27

I ask the Father in his great glory to give you the power to be strong in spirit. He will give you that strength through his Spirit. I pray that Christ will live in your hearts because of your faith. I pray that your life will be strong in love and be built on love.

—Ephesians 3:16–17

The Light shines in the darkness. And the darkness has not overpowered the Light.

—John 1:5

The way of the good person is like the light of dawn. It grows brighter and brighter until it is full daylight.

—Proverbs 4:18

Scripture Index

JESUS TODAY FOR KIDS

Sarah Young's devotional writings are personal reflections from her daily quiet time of Bible reading, praying, and writing in prayer journals. With sales of more than 14 million books worldwide, *Jesus Calling*® has appeared on all major bestseller lists. Sarah's writings include *Jesus Calling*®, *Jesus Today*®, *Jesus Lives*™, *Dear Jesus*, *Jesus Calling*® *for Little Ones*, *Jesus Calling*® *Bible Storybook*, *Jesus Calling*®: *365 Devotions for Kids*, and *Peace in His Presence*—each encouraging readers in their journey toward intimacy with Christ. Sarah and her husband were missionaries in Japan and Australia for many years. They currently live in the United States.

Jesus Calling® was written to help people connect not only with Jesus, the living Word, but also with the Bible—the only infallible, inerrant Word of God. Sarah endeavors to keep her devotional writing consistent with that unchanging standard. Many readers have shared that Sarah's books